Search Out the Land

A HISTORY OF AMERICAN MILITARY SCOUTS

ILLUSTRATED WITH PHOTOS AND MAPS

Search Out the Land

A HISTORY OF AMERICAN MILITARY SCOUTS

by Lieutenant Colonel Phillip H. Stevens
UNITED STATES ARMY

 RAND MCNALLY & COMPANY
Chicago · New York · San Francisco

To Steve
A good scout who
is still searching out the land

Contents

Acknowledgments

No book that purports to be a history can be the product of a single individual. The writer must have help from the people who are best qualified to keep him on the right track. This sort of help was provided to me by many people, many of whom were probably unaware of the purpose of my curiosity. These people provided access to the records in the National Archives, the Office of the Chief of Military History, Department of the Army, the Army Library, and, strangely enough, the Navy Library.

I owe a particular debt to Mrs. Edna Curcio, Photo Researcher for the Office of the Chief of Information, Department of the Army, for unflagging interest and patience with my problems. The staff of the Photo Library, Army Photographic Agency, consistently extended its cooperation beyond the limits of day-to-day duty. Mrs. Mary O'Brien, my version of the perfect secretary, helped in a variety of ways shuffled among the constant flow of paperwork in a busy office. Mrs. Lillian McClintock, and also Mrs. Margaret Stephens of Rand McNally, proved to me that editors are real and serve a worthwhile purpose.

To Kathleen, my understanding and patient wife, goes the credit for encouragement, criticism, and the drudgery of manuscript typing. We have made the book together.

The author and publisher wish to thank the following for permission to use illustrations: U.S. Signal Corps in the National Archives, pages 14(2), 31(2), 45, 101, 111, 137, 145; Office of the Chief of Military History, U.S. Army, page 65; U.S. Army Photos, pages 72, 77, 163, 181.

Illustrations and Maps

Introduction

And Moses sent them to spy out the land of Canaan, and said unto them, Get you up this way southward, and go up into the mountain:

And see the land, what it is; and the people that dwelleth therein, whether they be strong or weak, few or many;

And what the land is that they dwell in, whether it be good or bad; and what cities they be that they dwell in, whether in tents or in strongholds . . .

So they went up, and searched out the land from the wilderness of Zin unto Rehob . . .

Numbers 13:17–21

Nothing can upset the battle plans of a military leader faster than the arrival of an unexpected body of enemy troops, or finding himself in terrain that is too rough to permit his planned maneuvers. Moses wisely sought to avoid the unexpected by sending a small body of men ahead of the Children of Israel into the Land of Canaan. They "searched out the land" and gave Moses information which helped him make his plans.

The history of warfare seems to overlook the instances in which good information brought success, concentrating instead on the many examples of failure caused by the absence of timely intelligence. In 1813 an allied army of Russians and Prussians was seeking to destroy the Army of France, which had been weakened by Napoleon's defeat in Russia. In their haste to destroy the French, the allies failed to get enough information about Napoleon's location, and were not ready when they finally found him. Napoleon's soldiers were

8

gathered around their cook pots, preparing to lunch on chickens and potatoes gathered from the countryside, when the allies stumbled onto them. The French quickly rallied and, after a long and bloody battle, decisively defeated the attackers.

The man who goes ahead of an army in order to provide its commander with information is popularly called a "scout." The word is derived from the Latin verb *auscultare,* meaning "to listen." Over the years it has taken on deeper meaning and has come to describe a man who is skilled in many military arts. In the United States it has even broader significance because it has been traditionally applied to men who were wise in the ways of nature and of the great American frontier. When we think of American scouts, we picture such men as Robert Rogers, Kit Carson, and Buffalo Bill Cody. At some time during their lives they were all military scouts —skilled soldiers as well as accomplished frontiersmen.

Is a scout a spy? Certainly not! A scout goes about his business as a readily identifiable soldier, relying on his ability to elude the enemy and return with his information rather than depending on a disguise or false cover to conceal his true identity. Webster's dictionary sets it straight:

Scout: one sent to obtain information, especially a soldier . . . sent out in war to reconnoiter.

Spy: one who acts in a clandestine manner or on false pretenses to obtain information in the zone of operations of a belligerent . . . .

In the little *Handbook for Scouts,* written in 1912, Captain H. J. McKenney of the Twelfth United States Cavalry describes the information most necessary to a commander:

(1) The strength, intentions, positions, resources, morale, etc., of the enemy.

(2) The topography of the country.

(3) The resources of the country.

All these things, said Captain McKenney, must be found out not by spies, but by the troops themselves and, more specifically, by the scouts. These men, in his opinion, must be paragons of soldierly virtue: They must be physically strong; they must have good moral habits; they need to be well versed in reading, writing, and arithmetic; they must have good memories; they must learn quickly and observe accurately; they must be determined to carry out their mission even against seemingly insurmountable odds; and their fidelity, truthfulness, and physical courage must be unquestioned. As an afterthought, Captain McKenney added that they must be aware that a dead scout is of no value to anyone. Their mission has failed if they do not return alive with the desired information.

Scouts do not always operate alone. More frequently, they operate in small groups to provide security and the ability to make a fighting withdrawal, should they be discovered. Rogers' Rangers often went on scouting missions in the strength of several companies. But whether the scouting is done by one man or a hundred, the mission is the same—to get the information and get back with it.

This book tells the story of some military scouts who have added luster to the history of the United States. The story begins before the United States existed and includes the feats of men who, at the time of their most spectacular achievements, were in rebellion against the United States. It will describe the progress of scouts from buckskin-clad, flintlock-shooting woodsmen to the modern soldier-scout who rides a helicopter instead of a horse.

It is hoped that this historical progression will show that a scout today has the same basic purpose as his predecessors had in the days of the early frontier—to search out the land.

P.H.S.

1

Rogers' Rangers

Robert Rogers, first of the great American scouts, grew up on a New Hampshire farm in the middle of the eighteenth century, when the threat of attack by Indians was always present. A cautious farmer always had his rifle within reach, and if there was any advance warning of danger, he would quickly move his family into the comparative safety of the log fort he and the other settlers in the area had built. Sometimes the families would be forced to stay within the cramped quarters of the fort for weeks, until the marauding Indians got tired and went back to the deep woods, or until the New Hampshire militia drove them away.

By the time he was fourteen, Robert had developed a strong dislike for being cooped up in a log fort. The next time there was an Indian alarm, he joined the volunteers who went out to hunt them. For the rest of his life he seldom stayed long in a particular location.

Old records describe Rogers as a large, powerful man. He was not handsome, but his piercing eyes and persuasive manner offset his lack of good looks. He could read and write and had enough contact with educated town people to learn fair manners and courtesy.

For the ten years following his first military expedition, Robert Rogers did little but roam the wilderness. When his father bought him a farm, Robert found a tenant to run it and went back to the woods. Up to that point in life he had done nothing to distinguish himself except to be charged with passing counterfeit money. (His popularity and the public's indifference to counterfeiting saved him from trial.) But his roamings and his personality made him well known in New Hampshire, so when the bloody fighting of the French and Indian War (1754–60) began, it is not surprising that he was chosen to raise a company of militia.

In the winter of 1755–6, neither the French nor the English were very eager for serious military engagements. Both armies were engaged in improving their positions along Lake George and Lake Champlain. The French were completing Fort St. Frederick at Crown Point and Fort Carillon (known to the English as Fort Ticonderoga) at the southern end of Lake Champlain. These two forts commanded the passage between the lakes. Whoever occupied them could prevent an enemy from moving sizable forces by water northward into Canada or southward into the British colonies.

The English army spent the winter at Fort William Henry guarding the southern end of Lake George and access to the Hudson River. Although Rogers' frontiersmen had no official status in the British military system, they were sent out at least eight times that winter to gather information about the French. It is forty miles as the crow flies between Fort William Henry and Fort Ticonderoga, and still another five miles to Crown Point. They could not travel as the crow flies, in a straight line, but had to choose between rowing up the lake in plain sight of any observers or making their way overland through the snow. On most of these scouting trips (which Rogers called "scouts") he used a combination of these means—traveling as far as he could by boat, hiding the craft on the shore, and going the rest of the way on foot.

On December 19 Rogers, with three of his men, rowed up Lake George toward Ticonderoga. They rowed about fifteen miles that day, then landed, hid their boat, and spent the night. On December 20 they progressed about twenty miles overland and, as Rogers reports in his journal, "camped in a Pleasant Place between two Mountains, nothing remarkable happened this day."

By noon on December 21 they were in sight of Ticonderoga, and Rogers estimated that there were five hundred French troops in the fort. He and his fellow scouts set up an ambush in the hope of getting a prisoner, but each time the French ventured out of the fort they were in groups too big for Rogers' party to handle. As dark fell, the winter cold became unbearable and Rogers moved his men into an abandoned shed outside the fort. An early morning snowstorm forced them to give up their attempt to capture a prisoner since the new snow made traveling difficult while making it easier for the French and the Indian scouts to follow their trail. They were not able to reach their boat that day, so they camped and "lay in fear of pursuit." The next day they made their way back to Fort William Henry in time to celebrate Christmas.

By January 14 Lake George was frozen over and Rogers was able to change his way of traveling. He and seventeen of his men strapped on ice skates and skimmed northward over the ice. In the early afternoon of the second day they had reached the narrow neck of land that separates Lake George from Lake Champlain. They rested until dark, ate a cold meal, then crossed overland to the shores of Lake Champlain.

On ice again, they skated past the lights of Fort Ticonderoga to a point of land which juts out into the lake so far that any party of Frenchmen traveling between Crown Point

Map of Lake George area of New York, about 1750, showing forts William Henry, Ticonderoga, and Crown Point

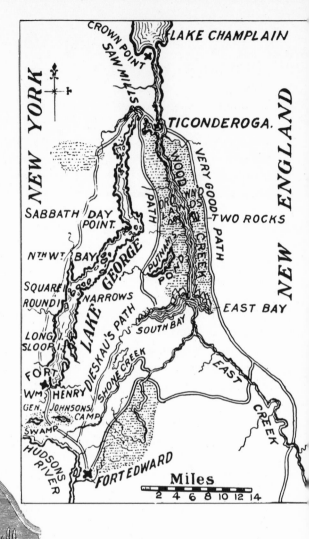

Robert Rogers, about 1760, when he was an Indian agent and a trader

and Ticonderoga would have to come within musket range. Their patience was rewarded shortly after sunrise by the appearance of two Frenchmen with a horse-drawn sled. The startled French, who were carrying fresh beef to Fort Ticonderoga, were quickly captured. Rogers and his companions started to make off with the sled and its load, but they were observed from Crown Point and a large party of soldiers was sent out to catch them. The rangers reluctantly killed the horse, dropped the whole rig through a hastily chopped hole in the ice, and got away. With their prisoners in tow, the scouts skated boldly back past Ticonderoga and reached Fort William Henry on the seventeenth—just three days after they had departed.

Nine days later, Colonel Glasier, the British commander at Fort William Henry, ordered Rogers and his company back to Crown Point for another look at the French. The written order provides an insight into the role the scouts were playing:

> Sir, you are hereby ordered to march the party under your command the nighest and best way you can to Crown Point. Then take a view of that fortress and outworks and make minutes of the same. If you meet Indians or any enemies on your way, you are to take them prisoners, or kill them, or distress them in any other way or means your prudence shall direct. . . . If you discover any large bodies of the enemy, you are to send one of the most active of your men with intelligence to me. . . .

The value of Rogers' men and the information they provided for the British commanders finally received formal recognition on May 23, 1756, when William Shirley, governor of Massachusetts and commander of all the British forces in North America, commissioned Rogers "to be Captain of an Independent Company of Rangers to be forthwith raised and Employ'd . . . ."

Rogers' men were not the first American military group to be called "rangers." About ten years earlier the General Assembly of New York had raised "new levies to range the woods," and in 1747 the New York assembly had passed a bill providing for "One Hundred Rangers" to be used in protecting the outlying settlements.

Rogers was authorized to enlist sixty privates to be paid three shillings a day, four sergeants at four shillings, an ensign (a sort of junior lieutenant) at five shillings, and two lieutenants at seven shillings. Captain Rogers was to be paid ten shillings a day. The Crown also authorized Rogers to spend ten Spanish dollars to clothe, equip, and arm each man.

Though Rogers' company was still not considered part of the regular British military establishment, their commission came from the Crown and they were subject to the discipline of the regular army, which raised them above the lowly status of provincial troops. Despite their position as troops of the Crown, Rogers' Rangers were a nondescript lot in appearance. They had no uniforms, so each man dressed in his favorite type of costume for "ranging the woods." Each ranger carried a musket, a tomahawk, and a scalping knife. His powder was carried in a bullock's horn slung from the left shoulder; the lead shot was in a pouch worn at the waist. Officers had a small compass set into the base of their powder horns.

Most colonial militia units were trained in formal, parade-ground drill which, except for instilling some appreciation for discipline, was of questionable value on the frontier. Rogers' Rangers were trained to follow a set of rules—a "Plan of Discipline" which their leader developed. These rules constitute Rogers' most lasting contribution to the American military tradition and are still used today by the United

States Army in training modern-day rangers. The twenty-eight rules he listed in his journal describe how a small unit of scouts should operate away from the main army. (*See* Appendix for fourteen of the rules.) Rogers outlined the way in which scouts were to maintain their equipment to be ready for instant action, the way in which scouts were to approach an enemy force without being discovered, and the formations they were to take "to keep one bullet from killing two men." The rules also instructed the rangers to position forward, flank, and rear guards to avoid being surprised while on the march, described how they were to handle prisoners to get the maximum amount of intelligence from them, and instructed them to disperse when in danger of being overwhelmed by a superior enemy force. Rogers summed up his rules with the caution, "there are, however, a thousand occurrences and circumstances which may happen that will make it necessary in some measure to depart from them and to put other arts and stratagems in practice."

Observers in the British camp reported seeing Rogers' men practicing the various maneuvers for hours on end. It is not surprising that the rangers could create panic in the ranks of the French by appearing, seemingly out of nowhere, firing a few devastating volleys, and then disappearing.

Once, while on a scout from Fort William Henry with two of his companies, Rogers was the fortunate beneficiary of his own training. His force was in search of a large number of Indians who had been employed by the French to raid English settlements and harass the British army. The wily Indians turned the tables on Rogers and ambushed his men deep in the forest, about fifteen miles from the fort.

The silence of the shady woods disappeared in a wild confusion of shots, shouts, screams, and Indian war cries. Rogers' men fought hand to hand with knives and tomahawks, but they were badly outnumbered. The shrill sound of the captain's whistle gave the prearranged signal for every ranger to break away on his own and escape. Rogers, too, turned and ran—but not quite fast enough!

A sharp pain seared his shoulder as the blunt end of a thrown tomahawk struck and knocked him to the ground. Instantly a muscular Indian was on him, trying to sink his knife where the tomahawk had missed. Rogers, in spite of the tomahawk blow, struggled with the brave and finally threw him to the ground. But as Rogers turned to continue his flight, the Indian grabbed him by his long hair. Rogers felt his scalp being drawn taut and his eyes bulging in their sockets. Just as he expected the scalping knife to strike, his hair slipped out of the Indian's hand. The leader of the rangers didn't dare take time to fight any longer. He ran the fifteen miles to the fort with the Indians in hot pursuit. Safely back among friends, Rogers gave thanks for his strength and for the bear grease he always used to dress his hair.

When reports of Rogers' tactics reached England, they were studied by the British army headquarters. Many regular officers of the British army considered Rogers' plan of discipline outright heresy. The twenty-eight rules flew in the face of military tradition, which still called for troops to advance across the battlefield in parade-ground fashion, their brilliantly colored uniforms and shiny buttons making perfect targets for anyone who took the trouble to aim his musket. But the Duke of Cumberland, captain general of the British army, finally had to give some credit to the rangers' continued success. He wrote to Lord Loudoun, the new British commander in America, and paid the frontier tactics a barbed compliment:

> Teach your troops to go out upon Scouting Parties; for 'till *Regular* Officers with men they can trust, learn to beat

the woods, & to act as *Irregulars*, you will never gain any certain Intelligence of the Enemy, as I fear, by this time you are convinced *Indian* Intelligence & that of *Rangers* is not atall to be depended upon. [The italics are the duke's.]

Recognition for Rogers was less grudging in America. He now had nine companies of rangers, and Lord Loudoun had permitted him to increase each company's strength from sixty to one hundred privates. They had uniforms—green coats to mark them as woodsmen, brown leggings buttoned up to the thigh, and, of course, moccasins on their feet. When on parade the rangers wore tricorn hats, but on a scout they preferred the Scottish tam-o'-shanter, a forerunner of the beret.

Lord Loudoun's last official act before returning to England was to confirm a promise he had made to promote Rogers to major. Loudoun's successor, Lord Howe, appointed Robert Rogers "Major of the Rangers in his Majesty's Service, and likewise Captain of a Company of Rangers."

When the war between the British and the French was over, Rogers' status was more or less unchanged. His rangers had made decisive contributions to all the British campaigns, and Rogers had the biggest independent command in the British army, but he was still only a major and was looked down upon by most of the British regulars as nothing more than a precocious provincial.

In 1763, during Chief Pontiac's bloody war against the white settlers to the west, Rogers regained some of his fame by participating in the relief of Detroit, which had been under siege by Pontiac's warriors for several months. By this time Rogers had begun to have visions of a fur trading empire in the West. These ambitions led to conflict with the British authorities and finally to a court-martial for treason and disobedience. Rogers was acquitted of the charges, but his reputation was left in question. He went to England in

1770 in an attempt to get back in the good graces of the British government, but succeeded only in being thrown into debtors' prison. Later he served briefly in the army of the Dey of Algiers and returned to America in 1775 as the rumblings of revolution began to grow louder.

Rogers was torn between his love of America and his loyalty to England. He had been drinking heavily for years, and this befuddling habit did not make it easy to come to a decision. He seemed to want to go in both directions at once. He wrote to George Washington, offering his services, but was suspected of treachery since he was still a half-pay officer in the British army. The suspicion of the American patriots finally drove him to offer his services to Lord Howe. The Americans arrested Rogers, but he escaped and made his way to the British.

With permission from the Crown and a commission as a lieutenant colonel, Rogers formed the Queen's Rangers, a regiment of American loyalists. Much to his disgust, however, it was converted into a regular infantry regiment. He asked to be relieved of his command of the Queen's Rangers and to be permitted to form a new ranger unit. Although permission was given, the new unit was formed very slowly. Rogers was now almost constantly in trouble over his drinking and his misuse of recruiting bounties. His efforts to find recruits were poorly organized and unenthusiastic.

With the Revolution over, Rogers was not wanted by either side. He returned to England and lived the rest of his life in a drunken fog, supported by his half-pay. The first of the great American scouts died in a London rooming house in 1795. In the years since his death, however, his military accomplishments have rightly come to overshadow his later misfortune, and his Plan of Discipline, though refined over the years, is still the basis for scouting techniques and formations used today by the United States Army.

2

Washington's Ranger

August 6, 1775, in Cambridge, Massachusetts, was the kind of hot summer day that drives boys into the protective arms of friendly shade trees and makes their dogs take panting shelter under convenient porches.

No one, not even soldiers, moved about in the afternoon heat, and the boys of Cambridge were probably startled when they saw the column of dusty men moving up the road into town. The boys very likely guessed that these lean men in buckskin suits, carrying the long rifles of frontiersmen, had come to join General Washington's army, but what a group! Sweat made muddy rivulets through the dust on their faces, and their buckskins clung to their backs, yet they walked with long, effortless strides.

The ninety-six men in the dusty column were the first troops from Virginia to join the growing army of their fellow Virginian, George Washington. Under the cajoling, driving, and even, now and then, beatings from their captain, they had marched the six hundred miles from Frederick County, Virginia, to Cambridge in just twenty-two days! Now the captain, Daniel Morgan, strode among his men, urging them to stand tall and sharp as they reached their goal.

The Cambridge boys must have been skeptical of a company that could have such an undistinguished-looking leader. Morgan dressed just as his men did and was every bit as sweat-streaked and dirty. There was no question about his ability in the minds of the Virginia riflemen, though. By frontier standards, Morgan was well suited to command.

Morgan had arrived in the Virginia backwoods in 1753 as a runaway boy of seventeen. He had worked on a farm, managed a sawmill, and hired himself out as a wagon driver. He had an almost unexcelled record as a powerful rough-and-tumble wrestler. Morgan was gentle and even magnanimous with defeated wrestling opponents, but on the rare occasions in which he lost a match he would sulk and brood over his victor's weak points until the chance came for a return bout. He never lost to the same man twice.

In 1755 the young wagon master had answered the call to provide transportation for General Braddock's army in its campaign to turn back the French invasion from the valley of the Ohio. Twenty-year-old Daniel Morgan had a rough introduction into the ways of soldiering. A British officer somehow triggered his quick temper and Morgan knocked him down. He was sentenced to receive four hundred lashes. The scars of that lashing were borne on Morgan's broad shoulders for the rest of his life, and his resentment at his treatment by the British may have been a reason for his haste to get to Cambridge twenty years later.

Morgan was present when Braddock lost both his army and his life at the hands of the French and Indians. In later years he often told of the horror of watching Braddock's redcoats and colonial militiamen trying to fight a parade-ground battle against an enemy hidden behind rocks and trees. He recalled having seen Colonel George Washington of the militia galloping back and forth across the battlefield trying to organize a withdrawal.

By 1773 Daniel Morgan was a well-established farmer near Winchester, Virginia, and had married Abigail Curry, a "plain, sensible, and pious" woman who educated Daniel and their two daughters.

On June 14, 1775, the Continental Congress voted to raise ten companies of "expert rifflemen." Six were to come from Pennsylvania and two each from Maryland and Virginia. Daniel Morgan was chosen by the prominent citizens of Frederick County to lead one of the Virginia companies, and since the Congress had authorized the levy, Morgan became a captain in the Continental army rather than in the Virginia militia.

Old records tell how Morgan saddled his horse each morning and rode around the county buttonholing potential recruits and describing the glory to be found in the defense of liberty. The new captain was a good recruiter. No record shows the exact method Morgan used to choose his men, but it seems that he was very particular to take only the best applicants. One captain of a rifle company, in a similar quandary, made the choice by drawing a man's nose on a board, placing this target 150 yards away, and taking the sharpshooters who came closest to hitting it. Whatever the method Morgan chose, his company soon exceeded the authorized strength of eighty-two men. This overstrength was later brought to the personal attention of General Washington, who had to find money to pay the extra men.

The boys in Cambridge, that hot August day in 1775, saw Morgan's Virginians hurrying to join the army around Boston less than two months after Congress had requested the troops.

Shortly after arriving, moved either by patriotic zeal or utter boredom over the lack of activity around Boston, Morgan volunteered his men to be part of an army preparing to invade Canada. He soon formed a fast friendship with the expedition commander, a former Connecticut apothecary named Benedict Arnold.

The invasion of Canada was designed to drive the British from that convenient base and to establish Canada as a fourteenth independent colony. As Washington conceived the invasion, Colonel Arnold's small army of about one thousand men was to make its way by sea to Gardiner, Maine, and finish its preparations at Fort Western, near the present site of Augusta. They would then move up the Kennebec and Dead rivers, over the mountains into Canada, and down the Chaudière River to Quebec. A second army, under Major General Philip Schuyler, was to take the traditional and easier route up Lake Champlain to the Sorel River and down the St. Lawrence. If all went according to plan, both armies would meet at Quebec.

Trouble settled on Arnold's little army before it left Fort Western. Arnold had intended to attach two of his companies of frontier riflemen to battalions commanded by officers of colonial militia. The riflemen, led by Morgan, protested that they could be commanded only by Continental officers. Since there were only two men in the expedition who fitted this qualification—Morgan and Arnold himself—Arnold was forced to put all three companies of riflemen under Morgan. Later, when General Washington heard that Morgan had claimed this had been Washington's specific intent, the general wrote his fellow Virginian a stinging letter denying any such instructions: Morgan and his men, he said, would serve under any superior officer, Continental or militia.

Morgan and the rifle companies set out from Fort Western on September 25, 1775, to move ahead of the body of the army scouting the route. Traveling in heavy, badly built bateaux (the flat-bottomed boats that were ordinarily used only on the lower part of the river), Morgan's men made very slow and difficult progress over the rapids and around the falls of the upper Kennebec. The green lumber that had been used for building the boats became waterlogged and split open, soaking the supplies.

By the time the rifle companies crossed into Canada the men were exhausted, and only Morgan's own company still had all seven of its boats. A member of the expedition wrote that Morgan's men had the flesh "worn from their shoulder, even to the bone" by the work of dragging the bateaux over the mountains. With their food gone, the men ate dogs, cooked their shot pouches, and even boiled their shaving soap and lip salve to render out the fat. Perhaps worst of all, one complete battalion of militiamen voted to quit the expedition and return home.

A relief force with flour, oatmeal, and cattle reached the army on November 2. The starving men immediately slaughtered the animals and many of them devoured the meat raw. By November 10 they had crossed the already frozen floodplain of the St. Lawrence and were at the river. The next day one of Morgan's advance scouts sighted a small group of British sailors on the river. The minor engagement that followed produced only a single prisoner, who would not divulge any worthwhile information, and the sailors who escaped warned Quebec of the presence of the revolutionary troops.

On the night of November 13, Arnold moved his men across the river. Their crossing was discovered by a British patrol boat, and most of Arnold's officers advised against an immediate assault on the city. Morgan, however, argued for an attack at once, before Quebec's defenses could be prepared. To demonstrate the enemy's lack of preparation, he led his men up the edge of the bluff and captured some sleepy British soldiers in a house outside the city wall. Temporarily encouraged by this success, Arnold marched his tattered army up and down outside the city, hoping to draw the garrison out into open combat, but they drew only the shouted insults of the soldiers and inhabitants. Arnold decided to withdraw until General Schuyler and his army, which had not been heard from in several weeks, arrived.

When the two revolutionary armies finally met on December 2, Brigadier General Richard Montgomery had replaced Schuyler. The combined forces, now under Montgomery, amounted to only 975 men. On December 4 Montgomery sent Morgan to reconnoiter near Quebec. Learning that the enemy was comfortably housed, well supplied, and assured of reinforcement early in the spring, Montgomery decided to attack immediately, before winter diminished his own force even more.

While Montgomery deployed his men, Morgan's riflemen sniped at the British defenders, and the American "artillery," consisting of a single six-pounder mounted on a sled, began to chip away at the massive stone walls of the city.

Before the assaulting colonials could even reach the walls, Arnold was wounded. An on-the-spot election was held and Morgan was appointed to take command of Arnold's part of the force, despite the fact that he was not next in seniority.

Morgan led his men up the first scaling ladder only to be tumbled back to the ground by a blast of fire from the British. Stunned, and blackened by powder burns, Morgan gathered his wits and began climbing again. This time he and his men made it over the top of the wall and into the streets of the city. They had momentary success, and Morgan felt they could take the city if Montgomery could reinforce him as planned. He did not know that Montgomery had already been killed before he had even reached the wall. The British commander fought coolly, gave ground where he had to, and attacked where he could. In the end the colonials had lost one hundred men killed or wounded and four hundred captured, while the British had lost only twenty. Morgan was among the prisoners.

While Arnold and the remnants of the army spent a miserable winter outside the city, Morgan and his fellow prisoners were given good treatment by the British. In May 1776 Arnold retreated from Quebec, arriving at Fort Ticonderoga in June. The prisoners were released in September.

Reports of Morgan's fine performance on this unfortunate expedition had been reaching General Washington for some time. Washington probably had also had personal discussions with Arnold, who greatly admired his former ranger commander. Washington recommended to John Hancock, president of the Continental Congress, that Morgan be promoted to colonel and given command of a regiment. Daniel Morgan was resting at his home in Winchester when the news came that he was appointed "Colonel of the Eleventh Regiment of Virginia, in the Army of the United States, raised for the defense of American liberty, and for repelling every hostile invasion thereof."

But Morgan, though as popular and persuasive as ever, had great difficulty in building a regiment. While he had been away on the Canadian expedition, many other recruiters had been through Virginia, and most of the good men already had been mustered into other regiments. Also, there was a growing shortage of rifles, and Morgan did not want to enlist men who could only be equipped with smoothbore muskets, which were not as accurate. Six months after he was commissioned to raise the regiment, Morgan had been able to muster only 180 men.

A letter from Congress urged Morgan to take his men and join Washington. "Let them bring what arms, blankets and clothes they have, or can by any means obtain . . . ," the letter instructed. A personal letter to Morgan from Patrick

Henry seconded the insistence with, "There is more pushing necessity for your aid than you are acquainted with . . . ."

When Morgan finally arrived at Washington's headquarters near Middlebrook, New Jersey, the general was so desperate for experienced rangers to watch the movements of the British that he directed Morgan to take his pick of officers and men from other regiments to form an elite "Corps of Rangers." They were to be dressed in the traditional buckskins of the frontier and armed with rifles. Morgan's first mission was assigned in a letter from General Washington:

> Head Quarters, Middle Brook, June 13, 1777
>
> Sir: The Corps of Rangers, newly formed, and under Your Command, are to be considered as a body of light Infantry and are to Act as such; for whh. reason they will be exempted from the common duties of the line.
>
> At present you are to take Post at Van Veghten Bridge and watch, with very small Scouting Parties (to avoid fatiegueing your Men too much, under the prest. appearance of things) the Enemys left Flank, and particularly the Roads leading from Brunswick toward Millstone, or have your retreat to the Army cut off.
>
> . . . It occurs to me that if you were to dress a Company or two of true Woods Men in the right Indian Style and let them make the Attack accompanied with screaming and yelling as the Indians do, it would have very good consequences especially if as little as possible was said, or known of the matter beforehand.

Almost immediately, Morgan's forward scouts brought word that a British column had moved out of Brunswick during the night and had reached Somerset Courthouse before being discovered. This news was swiftly sent to Washington while Morgan, just as swiftly, prepared to harass the enemy's flanks.

The rangers opened fire on the column and kept up a steady rattle of well-aimed shots. Under this pressure the British ranks began to thin, as men either dropped from wounds or took cover along the side of the road. Many of those who left the road regretted it, as they became easy game for the scalping knives and tomahawks of the stalking rangers. Everything seemed to go well. The rangers, eager for more action, began to flow out of the woods to attack the main body of the column.

At first this assault appeared to succeed, but the British by now had had time to move artillery forward and fire several blasts. The rangers were not prepared to cope with that kind of punishment and began to break off the engagement, filtering back into the woods. Luckily they suffered only a few casualties, but the departure from their instructions to avoid decisive combat brought a gentle rebuke from Washington, who was apparently too pleased with the action to react more strongly.

Morgan's constant harassment was too much for the British commander, General Cornwallis, who decided that since the Americans would not meet him openly, it would be discreet to withdraw. The rangers pursued the redcoats and their allies all the way to Piscataway, giving their rear guard a very hard time.

While British General Howe was making a series of maneuvers designed to confuse Washington about his true intentions, another British army was taking action that left no doubt in anyone's mind. General "Gentleman Johnny" Burgoyne had captured Fort Ticonderoga with a mixed force of British, Germans, Tories, and Indians, and was threatening Albany. The influential patriots of upper New York were crying for help.

Although Washington was reluctant to release Morgan's men to go northward to help out in New York while he was still unsure about Howe's intentions, he finally agreed to send them on the condition that, if necessary, the rangers could be instantly recalled. He wrote to Governor Clinton of New York that Morgan's riflemen would cause wholesale desertions among Burgoyne's Indian raiders. He further advised Clinton, "I should think it would be well even before their arrival to circulate these Ideas [that Morgan's riflemen were on the way], with proper Embellishments, throughout the Country, and in the army and to take pains to communicate them to the Enemy. It would not be amiss, among other Things, to magnify Numbers." George Washington was asking the governor of New York to do some purposeful lying.

On August 29, 1777, the rangers arrived at the junction of the Mohawk and Hudson rivers, just above Albany. That night Morgan dined with his new commander, Major General Horatio Gates, a former British regular and Morgan's neighbor from the valley of Virginia. Here, also, Morgan was reunited with his old friend Benedict Arnold.

Nine days later, on September 7, 1777, Gates sent Morgan and his rangers into action. Their mission was to move ahead to the American army and locate Burgoyne. Morgan found Burgoyne and his army collecting at Saratoga, preparing to advance on the American camp at Albany. They had followed the well-traveled invasion route from Canada down Lake Champlain to Ticonderoga and on to the Hudson River. The British crossed the Hudson on September 13 and 14 and four days later were within three miles of the American camp. Morgan had watched their movements and had reported each one to Gates, but Burgoyne had deprived himself of the means of securing similar intelligence about the Americans. His Indian scouts had been driven away by Burgoyne's harsh treatment of his Indian allies for violating orders against killing white women.

Despite his lack of information, on September 19 the

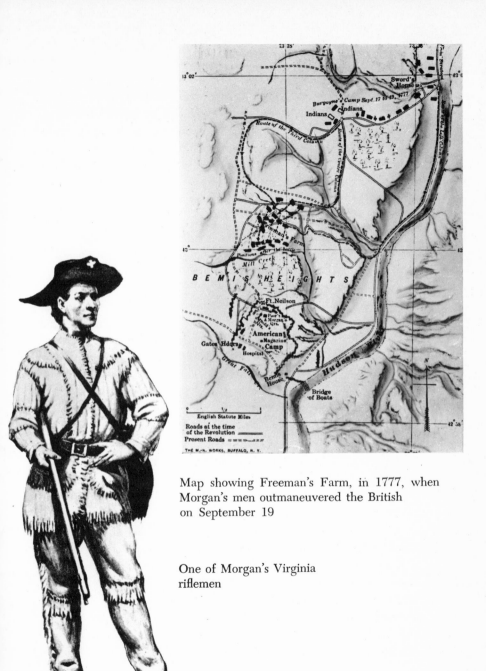

Map showing Freeman's Farm, in 1777, when
Morgan's men outmaneuvered the British
on September 19

One of Morgan's Virginia
riflemen

flamboyant and ever-confident Burgoyne decided to attack the Americans, who were sitting snugly in field fortifications designed by a Polish volunteer, General Thaddeus Kosciuszko. Even when the British troops were close enough to be seen from the American fortifications, General Gates seemed content to let them come on unimpeded. Benedict Arnold, already unhappy with Gates, urged him to send Morgan's men into the bordering woods to at least slow down the British advance. Gates reluctantly agreed, and the riflemen hurriedly moved to the left flank of the American position. They stationed themselves in the woods surrounding a large clearing known as Freeman's Farm.

It is not known whether Morgan's choice of this position was based on intelligence of Burgoyne's plans or was sheer happenstance, but the hidden riflemen watched with relish as Burgoyne's scarlet-coated advance guard, some three hundred strong, sauntered into the clearing and began to form ranks for the advance on the American position. The long rifle barrels were slowly raised and their sights brought to bear on the epaulets of the officers and the breastplates of the sergeants. The quiet tension was broken slightly by the soft gobble of a turkey call—Morgan's command to fire—and every British officer in the advance guard, save one, fell to the ground.

The British appeared to be in complete panic, so the irrepressible rangers once again left the security of the woods and tried to finish the job. They were not so lucky as they had been in New Jersey. Their path to safety was cut off by a quick flanking movement executed by General Fraser, the commander of Burgoyne's right wing. Watching helplessly, Morgan saw his lightly armed rangers recoil from the compressed ranks of the British regulars. He sounded his turkey call for a withdrawal and then sat down to moan, "I am ruined, by God! . . . and my men are scatted, God knows where!" It is the only recorded instance of Morgan's loss of composure during a battle.

Using the same plan of discipline as that followed by Rogers' Rangers, Morgan's riflemen fled from the battle and gathered again as a group. Reassured by the discovery that casualties had actually been rather light, Morgan again deployed his men so as to keep up a steady fire against the advancing British. When night fell, the redcoats were still a mile from the American fortifications. Of the 300 men who had marched out that morning with the British Sixty-second Regiment, only 97 were unhurt. About 1,100 British troops had actually made contact with the Americans that day and 600 of them were casualties. The entire American force, including Morgan's men, had 319 killed, wounded, or missing. Both Burgoyne and Gates reported victory to their superiors.

The exhausted armies rested and resupplied themselves for more than two weeks. Then, on October 7, Burgoyne, against the advice of his staff, decided to take the midcourse between retreat and attack. He ordered a reconnaissance in force by fifteen hundred men to probe the American positions. The ensuing battle was largely a repetition of the earlier one, except that the rangers did not try to engage the heavily armed British infantry. General Fraser, dashing gallantly back and forth across the battlefield, again almost saved the day for Burgoyne. Fraser's effect on the battle became so apparent to Morgan that he called a group of his best riflemen together and instructed them to bring Fraser down. Fraser's continuous movement saved him for a while, but the growing number of near misses warned him that he had been singled out. He refused to take cover and was finally mortally wounded. Just before he died, he reported that the man who had shot him was a rifleman, high in a tree.

Burgoyne wasted little time in starting a withdrawal

toward Fort Ticonderoga. Harassed every step of the way by the ever-present rangers, the British got as far as Saratoga before being surrounded and forced to surrender. When Burgoyne met Morgan, the dapper general took the backwoods colonel by the hand and said warmly, "Sir, you command the finest regiment in the world."

General Washington wanted the rangers to rejoin the main army, and to make sure that Gates would not delay their departure, he sent Colonel Alexander Hamilton to represent him. "Let them know how essential their services are to us," instructed Washington, "and desire the colonel . . . to hasten his march as much as is consistent with the health of his men after their late fatigues."

Morgan and his men reached Washington's headquarters at Whitemarsh, Pennsylvania, on November 18. The rangers were tired, many of them were sick, and all of them needed shoes, clothing, and blankets. Morgan himself was beginning to show the physical results of strenuous campaigning. As the weather grew colder, sciatica, which had begun to bother him in Canada, returned to make his every movement painful. Nevertheless, Morgan took the 160 sound rangers left in his corps and once again set out to scout the movements of the British.

Late in December, Washington moved his desperate army to Valley Forge. The area offered better defensive positions and blocked the supply route of the British to their garrison in Philadelphia. Morgan and his rangers were placed on the west side of the Schuylkill River to cut off the movement of supplies and to watch the British. Considering the miserable conditions under which they were forced to exist, the rangers did a remarkable job that winter, harassing supply trains, intercepting British spies and sympathizers traveling to and from Philadelphia, and plaguing any red-coated troops that ventured out of their warm winter quarters. During most of this time the ranger colonel was not with his men. The weather had almost completely crippled him and he had begged and been granted leave by Washington to return to his Virginia fireside.

The spring of 1778 brought more than just the promise of summer. On April 30 General Washington received word that France had recognized the independence of the American colonies. Though this act brought no immediate remedies for the general's host of problems, it did succeed in raising the morale of the army. By this time Morgan had returned from Virginia and the Corps of Rangers continued their patrolling and harassing during the balance of the spring. They were involved in this sort of activity on June 28, when they reconnoitered a British force based at Monmouth Courthouse, in New Jersey. The British commander, Sir Henry Clinton, decided that the time had come to get away from the harassment by the Virginia riflemen and began to move toward the safety of New York. Morgan started after him, but was stopped by a series of confusing orders from the American commander in the field, General Charles Lee. In the meantime, other American troops made contact with Clinton's troops, and a major battle developed. Still without specific orders, Morgan marched his men to the site of the battle, but arrived too late to have any effect. The battle of Monmouth was over. No clear victory could be claimed by either side, but Washington was furious over Lee's mishandling of the battle, and particularly over the absence of the rangers, whose assistance might have been decisive. Lee was ordered to the rear and was later court-martialed.

Washington sent the rangers hurrying after Clinton's rear guard. Morgan's men chased the British all the way to Sandy Hook, only to watch them set sail for New York. It was Morgan's last action as Washington's ranger, for his experience in battle was needed at a higher level. He was given command of a brigade, and, though the parting with his Virginia comrades was painful, Morgan now set his sights on becoming a general. He had a long wait.

In 1779, after a year of promises and frustration, with no promotion forthcoming, Morgan submitted his resignation to Congress. It was accepted, but was later changed to an extended leave of absence. After fifteen months at home he returned to duty to come to the assistance of his former commander, General Gates, who had just suffered a disastrous defeat at Camden, South Carolina. Eight days later, on October 15, 1780, an inconstant Congress promoted the onetime wrestling champion of Frederick County, Virginia, to the rank of brigadier general.

Morgan spent the rest of the war fighting in the south with regular troops, but he continued to apply the techniques he had used so effectively with his rangers. His greatest day came on January 17, 1781, when eight hundred Americans, a mixture of continentals and militia, met more than one thousand of the best British fighting men under Lieutenant Colonel Banastre Tarleton. The battle was fought on a grassy slope in Georgia called Hannah's Cowpens. The good marksmanship of the Continental troops combined with Morgan's inspired leadership to inflict a staggering blow to the pride of the British army. British casualties included 36 officers among the 100 British killed and an amazing total of 830 prisoners, 230 of whom were wounded. Tarleton fled from the battle of Cowpens with less than 200 men.

Morgan is most often remembered for this battle and not for the earlier years of service with his rangers. There is little doubt, however, that his greatest contribution to the military tradition of the new United States was the implanting of the frontier skills of marksmanship and scouting as integral parts of basic military tactics.

3

Robert E. Lee,
Engineer and Scout

On August 19, 1846, when the United States was preparing for war with Mexico, Captain Robert E. Lee, Corps of Engineers, United States Army, received a letter from the chief engineer in Washington ordering him to report to Brigadier General John E. Wool, in San Antonio de Bexar, Texas.

For Lee this order provided a final opportunity to escape from a heretofore mediocre career. He had begun his military service twenty-one years earlier when he entered West Point. In 1846, when the call to action finally came, he was almost forty years old, had never been in battle, and was already having visions of early retirement while many of his better-known contemporaries moved ahead in rank.

The journey to San Antonio took just two days more than a month. Lee reported to General Wool on September 21 and immediately plunged into the preparations for a move into Mexico. Wool's little army of 1,954 men moved out of San Antonio on September 28, with Captain Lee helping to supervise the pioneer troops who were working in advance of the column repairing roads and building bridges. Eleven days later the army crossed the Rio Grande on a pontoon bridge built by Lee's men.

The American troops were eager for their first clash with the Mexicans. Every report of an approaching enemy force started a feverish sharpening of bayonets and swords. But each rumor proved false, and General Wool became increasingly angry at each new cry of "Wolf!" Lee was standing at Wool's side one evening when a message was received that a large number of Mexicans were bearing down on Wool's small force. Lee asked to verify the report, and Wool sent him on the first of his many scouting missions in Mexico.

Setting out in darkness, with a Mexican boy as guide and interpreter, Lee quickly found the tracks of many wagons and mules along the road ahead of the American encampment. Although he could not find any deep ruts, which would indicate the presence of artillery, Lee assumed that other horse-drawn vehicles moving over the road had obliterated the cannon wheel marks. He was almost ready to return to Wool with a report that a sizable enemy force was just ahead, but decided to continue until he reached the outposts of the Mexican camp, in the hope of finding more evidence.

Lee and his young guide rode for several hours without being challenged. Finally they saw many campfires clustered on a hillside. The Mexican boy explained to Lee that there was a stream nearby, making this location an ideal campground for an army. He urged a hasty return to the American camp, but Lee told the boy to wait while he moved closer. Soon Lee could see what appeared to be a large number of white tents. He crossed the stream and came within earshot of loud talking and the typical rattling and clanking sounds of a camp. Again he almost bolted back to General Wool with confirmation of the enemy's presence, but he squinted one last time at the white tents—and saw that they moved! The "tents" were sheep and the "soldiers" were drovers moving the herd to market! Lee rode into the camp, and in halting Spanish asked the drovers the location of the Mexican army. They told him that it was "far away, over the mountains." Lee picked up his guide and returned to the American camp.

As engineer for an army that was hardly larger than a single brigade, Captain Lee had little opportunity to display the characteristics which later made him famous. He had to be content with the tasks that keep an army moving—building roads, repairing bridges, and locating campsites.

In January 1847 Lee's military horizons were broadened by orders to join the staff of General Winfield Scott, the commander of the entire expedition into Mexico. In the months that followed, Lee frequently showed his ability to scan the expected scene of a battle and to devise movements which took advantage of every bit of favorable terrain while minimizing the effects of obstacles. In the very best tactical and strategic sense, Captain Lee "searched out the land."

Less than two months after he had joined General Scott, Lee had risen to a point of considerable favor with "Old Fuss 'n Feathers." Despite his pomposity and love of ceremony, Winfield Scott was a capable commander and a shrewd judge of men. He made Lee a member of his "little cabinet" of staff officers.

While a fleet of American warships and troop transports waited at sea off the port city of Veracruz, Lee assisted in the reconnaissance of the city's fortifications and in the search for good landing beaches. Lee came under enemy fire for the first time during this reconnaissance, and again later while selecting firing positions for American artillery to be used in the siege of the city.

Three days of bombardment were enough for the Mexican defenders of Veracruz. General Scott arranged a brief but impressive ceremony for the surrender, sent the appropriate dispatches to Washington, and then set out for the interior of Mexico in search of the main Mexican army under General Antonio Santa Anna.

When American scouts found the enemy on April 13,

1847, Santa Anna and his men were waiting for them in a well-chosen defensive position along the National Road leading to Mexico City. The position was dominated by a peak known as Cerro Gordo. Scott knew he had either to find a way to get around the Mexicans or make a head-on attack against their formidable positions. He called on Lee to make a reconnaissance and to select flanking routes.

The Mexican right flank was protected by sheer cliffs which rose from a river. Lee ruled out this approach immediately. The left flank was guarded by a series of rugged ravines, but Lee set out to see if there was any possibility of moving through them.

Finding the ravines difficult but not impossible to traverse, he moved ever closer to the Mexican position on the higher ground. Pausing to catch his breath and to look around, he discovered that he had reached a spring which nestled in the hillside. Almost simultaneously he heard voices speaking Spanish and realized that the speakers were coming toward the spring. The only hiding place was behind the trunk of a dead tree which had fallen near the water.

Lee burrowed between the log and the grass which had grown up around it and lay still. From this hiding place he watched some Mexican soldiers approach the spring, drink deeply, and then settle down for a quiet chat in the coolness of the damp rocks. Finally the men got up and slowly walked away, but just as Lee was preparing to leave his sanctuary, another group of Mexicans appeared.

The day grew hotter and the insects that always infest a rotting tree found in Captain Lee a tasty change in their diet. His cramped muscles ached for the relief of movement. Each departing group of Mexicans was replaced by another. Some of them sat on the log, only a few inches from Lee's sweat-soaked back. One stepped over the log, almost using Lee's hidden leg as a stepping stone. The day wore on slowly and agonizingly, but twilight finally ended the procession of

Mexicans in search of a cool drink. Only when it was completely dark, however, did Lee crawl painfully out of his hiding place. With nothing more than his innate sense of direction to guide him, he groped his way through the moonless night until he reached the army camp.

Lee's report strengthened Scott's determination to go around the Mexican left flank, capture Cerro Gordo, and block the escape of Santa Anna's army. The next day Lee took a small party of pioneer troops back over the path he had used, avoiding the spring, of course, and they worked to make it passable for larger numbers of men. The job was done by sundown, and Lee was instructed by Scott to guide General Twiggs' division of regular army troops through the ravines and into the Mexican flank. Twiggs' men were simply to make the approach to the Mexican flank and then hold fast until Scott's main attack was launched the next day.

The first of the regiments of Twiggs' command had just reached the hilltop when they were discovered and attacked by a much larger force of Mexicans. Twiggs immediately ordered two more regiments forward. One company commander who did not understand precisely how far the attack was to be carried asked Twiggs, "I beg pardon, General, how far shall we charge them?" The peppery general replied, "Charge them to hell!" And that's just about what they did. The excited American regulars, in close combat with the Mexicans for the first time, drove the defenders backward out of their main positions and were halfway up the side of Cerro Gordo when Twiggs had the buglers sound "Recall" for fear his men would go too far.

The battle for Cerro Gordo was ended quickly the next day. More than three thousand Mexican soldiers were captured, together with a large store of arms. In his haste to escape, General Santa Anna had even left his money chest behind. General Scott showed his appreciation for Lee's work by writing to the War Department:

I am impelled to make special mention of the services of Captain R. E. Lee, engineers. This officer, greatly distinguished at the siege of Vera Cruz, was again indefatigable, during these operations, in reconnaissance as daring as laborious, and of the utmost value. Nor was he less conspicuous in planting batteries, and in conducting columns to their stations under the heavy fire of the enemy.

The secretary of war echoed Scott's praise by giving Captain Lee a brevet promotion (an honorary promotion with no increase in pay), to major, but the tortuous combination of War Department administration and slow mail kept this happy news from him for several months.

Scott and his army gradually made their way toward the Mexican capital without any major contest with the Mexican army. Scott assumed that Santa Anna was having difficulty reorganizing after the disaster at Cerro Gordo.

The two armies finally met again at San Augustin, a few miles south of Mexico City. Santa Anna had once more made clever use of the terrain to assist in his defense. The ground on his left flank was softened by the waters of Lake Xochimilco and was therefore impassable for artillery or heavy wagons. An attack on the left would have to be made by foot soldiers without artillery support. His right flank was screened by a vast field of viciously sharp lava rock known as the *pedregal*. A frontal attack, into the center of the Mexican position, would be costly and might fail. Captain Lee was once more sent out to find an alternative—a route to the Mexican right flank around or across the *pedregal*.

He set out with an escort of infantry and cavalry, and soon found that there was indeed a rough road at the edge of the lava, but just as he began to hope that the road had been left unguarded, a strong force of Mexicans opened fire. After a brief fight in which Lee's men took five prisoners, both forces broke off the engagement. Then Lee found a sort of peak in the lava field and climbed up to get a better view. He decided that the Americans could cross the western end of the *pedregal,* get behind the Mexican position, and have a clear path into the flank of the main Mexican defenses at San Augustin. After General Scott heard Lee's report, he decided to use this plan.

Following a route mapped out by Lee, a force of some 3,300 Americans got across the knife-sharp surface of the *pedregal* and into position to attack the secondary Mexican position guarding the road around the lava. But much to the consternation of the senior American officer, General Persifor F. Smith, they found a very large force of Mexicans (estimated by some observers to have as many as 12,000 men) arrayed for battle less than a mile ahead of them. Apparently unimpressed by the fighting qualities of the Mexican army, General Smith began to deploy his 3,300 men for an immediate attack on the 12,000!

It is difficult to guess what might have happened if night and a drenching rain had not interrupted Smith's preparations. Lee had informed General Scott of the situation during the afternoon and then had been sent back across the *pedregal* to General Smith in the evening rain. He conveyed Scott's confidence that Smith's men could hold off the main Mexican force while making the planned attack on the secondary position—the original objective. Smith altered his plans to coincide with Scott's pointed suggestion, and Lee went back to report Smith's intentions and dispositions to Scott. Lee heard Scott approve General Smith's plans and then set out again to make sure that the troops sent to support Smith's attack were properly positioned. In accomplishing this mission, he crossed the treacherous lava bed for a second time.

The battle that began at daybreak was the fiercest contest of the war. The Americans suffered more than 1,000 casualties, and the estimated loss in the Mexican ranks was more than 6,000, including 2,600 captured. The end of the fighting found the Americans at the gates of Mexico City.

Lee's part in the operation brought a veritable flood of praise from all the major commanders in Scott's expeditionary army. The commanding general later said that Lee's two painful trips across the *pedregal* on the night of August 19 were "the greatest feat of physical and moral courage performed by any individual, in my knowledge, pending the campaign." Eventually the praise was rewarded with another brevet promotion, to the honorary rank of lieutenant colonel. Lee did not become a regular lieutenant colonel for another eight years, and it took a transfer from the engineers to the cavalry to accomplish that promotion.

After the battle on the outskirts of Mexico City, the Mexicans sought an armistice, but on September 6, after thirteen days of inconclusive negotiations, Scott was convinced that agreement was not possible. He ordered preparations for an attack on the Mexican capital. Lee's first task was his usual one—reconnaissance of the defenses of the city. He reported to Scott that the city was situated on high ground surrounded by a plain which was usually flooded or very muddy during the rainy summer. A series of causeways crossed these bogs from the south and west. The causeways from the south were guarded by small defended positions while those from the west could be covered from the city itself and from the citadel of Chapultepec, a castlelike military school built on the crest of a ridge and surrounded by a brick wall.

Lee recommended an approach from the south, to avoid Chapultepec. Scott chose instead to attack from the west and to storm the citadel. The distance was shorter, and Scott did not believe the Mexicans would put up a serious fight for Chapultepec in the face of heavy bombardment by the American artillery. Lee's next task was to find sites for the heavy artillery so it could be used most effectively against the fortifications. By September 12, 1847, after two days of

The American infantry attacking Chapultepec on routes scouted by Robert E. Lee

hard work, Lee had four batteries of artillery in position and firing on Chapultepec.

Scott's plan called for a heavy bombardment of Chapultepec early in the morning, accompanied by a diversionary attack along the causeways in the south. At his command, the fire on the citadel would be lifted and the infantry regiments would begin their assault against the fortress walls.

The growing roar of the artillery firing in the morning haze heightened the excitement of the troops waiting to make the attack on Chapultepec. Tension continued to mount until the expected sudden silence of the guns gave them the signal to begin the assault. The troops walked, then trotted, then ran into the defending fire from the walls of Chapultepec. The scaling ladders went up, as they had centuries earlier in attacks against medieval castles. In the same medieval fashion, the first brave men up the ladders bore the brunt of the Mexican defensive weapons and fell back, to be replaced by another assault wave, and another. It seemed that the battle had hardly started when the American regimental flags were flying atop the walls.

The attack against Mexico City itself was pressed home the next day. By nightfall General Santa Anna had abandoned the city, and Scott marched in early in the morning on September 15. There was no more serious fighting. The first major American involvement in a war on foreign soil was at an end.

Lee, whose future had been seriously in doubt when he was ordered to Mexico in August 1846, established himself during the war as an outstanding engineer, staff officer, and reconnaissance expert. In 1861, when the Civil War was smoldering, General Scott, who at seventy-five was still on active duty as general-in-chief of the army, favored Lee above all others to command the forces that would put down the rebellion.

4

Kit Carson,
a Model for Americans

Of all the American folk heroes, Kit Carson probably comes closest to being the "ideal" frontiersman. He could track any quarry, animal or human, over the most difficult terrain and then bring it down with a single rifle shot. Astride a horse or a mule he seemed to become a part of the mount. When dealing with other men, whether they were Indians, Spaniards, or half-wild mountain trappers, Kit Carson spoke their language and understood their problems.

Kit Carson knew the ways of nature, and the habits of nature's creatures were his everyday stock-in-trade. He was inventive, courageous, and tenacious. He was a natural leader. When necessary, he could inspire men to outdo themselves. But he was also a quiet, humble man.

Christopher Carson was born in Daniel Boone country. His father admired Boone and may even have known him. In any event, Daniel Boone's call to the adventure of the frontier had lured the senior Carson from his homestead in West Virginia to the wilds of Kentucky. By the time Christopher joined the family on Christmas Day, 1809, there were already four older brothers, and the Carsons' little piece of Kentucky wilderness had been pretty well tamed. Christo-

pher became "Kit" almost at once. He was his mother's dar-
ling and the pet of his older brothers. They taught him to
ride and to shoot almost as soon as their mother taught him
to read and write (some of his biographers maintain that he
was illiterate but this is not true). Kit probably received
more than the youngest child's usual share of attention because he was physically a runt. He was a small boy who became a small man, but one who was a giant among his
physical superiors.

When Kit was five years old, his father again took up
the trail of Daniel Boone, this time to Howard County in
Missouri. This was real frontier country, where the settlers
lived in a log fort and worked their fields under constant
guard. The Missouri and Osage Indians were, quite under-
standably, resisting this encroachment on their prime hunting grounds, and Kit, like all the children old enough to
help in the fields, was taught to shoot first and ask questions
later. Indian resistance ended suddenly in that part of
Missouri when smallpox, a much more effective Indian killer
than the white man's rifle, decimated the tribes. Overnight
the frontier fort became a relic as the settlers moved out
onto their land to build real homes.

Now young Kit could roam the country at will. He
stalked deer and buffalo and hid himself in marsh grass to
wait for a shot at plump wild geese. He was friendly toward
the Indians who had survived the epidemic and was soon
able to speak both of the local Indian dialects. As he walked
the leaf-shaded trails of the Missouri woods, Kit worked to
refine the marksmanship skills taught him by his brothers.
He would pick out a distant leaf and then, pretending he
had been surprised by an enemy, would leap behind a tree
or a rock or simply throw himself flat on the ground, firing
at the hostile leaf from the new position. His brothers
thought these gymnastics uproariously funny, but the serious

Kit explained that you could not expect an enemy to wait while you assumed a proper shooting stance and took careful aim. At the age of twelve Kit was given his first horse, and he expanded his offhand shooting techniques to suit his new mobility, training himself to shoot from the saddle or while hanging under the horse's belly.

The high points of life on the Missouri frontier were the periodic jamborees that were held to celebrate almost any kind of an occasion. Families gathered from all over the country, traded for things they needed, caught up on all the latest gossip, ate a collective picnic banquet, and watched as their menfolk displayed their skills. Kit Carson and his oldest brother Moses were almost always the best marksmen in the competition, but it was the free-for-all fighting that got the most attention.

A free-for-all was a substitute for the duels or knife fights which had long been used to settle grudges or "affairs of honor." Several boys or men of about the same age would climb into a pit and engage in a no-holds-barred fight to see who would be the last one standing upright. No weapons were permitted, but gouging, biting, kicking, and butting were considered to be in the best of form. Kit was taunted into his first free-for-all in the summer of 1822, when he was thirteen. He planned his campaign carefully. He stood with his back against the wall of the pit and made his tormentors come at him one at a time. Once in contact, he fought furiously and effectively—so effectively, in fact, that he got overconfident and left the protection of the pit wall. Several boys instantly seized him, pummeled him severely, and threw him out of the pit.

That autumn, at another jamboree, Kit stuck to his original battle plan and emerged groggy but victorious. For the first time in his life he displayed the iron will and physical stamina that were to carry him through much adversity.

When Kit was sixteen, his father lost all hope of keeping him on the farm and apprenticed the lad to a saddlemaker in a nearby town. Kit did not like the work. He felt hemmed in by the walls of the shop and by the fence around the yard where the hides were cured and tanned. However, although he didn't realize it at the time, he was acquiring skills that would serve him well in later years.

The saddle shop was a favorite meeting place for trappers, wagon masters, and settlers on their way west. Kit learned the language of the trail and quickly picked up the names and functions of the most complicated wagon harness. He drank in all the tall tales told by men who had been to the plains of New Mexico, to the high Rockies, and to California.

Kit endured his apprenticeship for almost two years, and then joined a group of settlers bound for New Mexico. He had set his mind on being a trapper and on joining the exclusive company of "mountain men."

The journey to Santa Fe was uneventful, but Kit's dreams of quick success as a trapper were ended almost as soon as he arrived. The Mexican governor was doing his best to discourage American fur trapping and trading in the southern Rockies and would grant a license only if a prohibitively high license fee were paid. Many traders were moving out of Santa Fe, selling their precious traps and rifles to buy food. Kit kept himself going by doing any kind of a job he could find.

He broadened his knowledge of Indian dialects by learning those of the local tribes and, out of necessity, he also learned Spanish. Over the course of the next two years Kit developed a reputation as an eager, intelligent young man who was willing to work hard. He drove wagons, worked as a cook, and was occasionally hired as an interpreter, but he seldom had even enough money to buy clothes.

Finally, in the fall of 1829, in the little mountain town of Taos, Kit found the opportunity he sought. Ewing Young, a well-known fur trader, was organizing an expedition to punish a group of Indians who had ambushed five of his trappers, but was using this expedition to cover his real intent—to do some trapping without paying the Mexican license fee. Young hired Kit Carson as a sort of extra rifleman, thus rounding out his expedition to forty men.

There were probably three hundred Indians in the group they were after, but the disparity in numbers was more than balanced by the white man's greater skill in killing. Before the Civil War, few Indians had firearms and their skill with the bow and arrow depended largely on stalking their quarry and getting very close before taking a shot. The white hunters, to the contrary, were all armed with rifles and could bring down a deer, or an Indian, at two hundred yards or better.

Tracking such a large group of Indians was very easy for men whose livelihood depended on their ability to read signs made by small animals. The trappers cornered the Indians in the mountains near the junction of the Gila and Salt rivers (near the present site of Phoenix, Arizona), and killed fifteen of them. Kit Carson was credited with killing an Indian in this, his first battle, though his feelings on the subject were not recorded.

Having taken care of the Indians, Ewing Young immediately turned the attention of the expedition to the more important activity of fur trapping. The winter's trapping was highly successful, and even before the snows began to melt the party had acquired many bales of fine beaver pelts. Twenty-two of the men were sent back to Taos with the furs while Ewing Young, with the other seventeen men, including Kit Carson, set out for California and the Sacramento River valley to investigate its potential for fur trapping.

In April of 1830, after a successful winter of trapping in California spiced with a couple of serious encounters with Indian parties, Young and his men returned to Taos. The sale of their furs brought Kit Carson a thousand dollars, an almost unbelievable sum for a fledgling trapper. He headed for the more lively town of Santa Fe, and although the biography which he helped prepare says he "learned no bad habits," Kit Carson, twenty years old, trapper and Indian fighter, was broke by autumn.

Now that he was an accepted member of the family of mountain men, Kit had no trouble finding work that fall. It was the beginning of a ten-year period during which Kit established a reputation rivaling that of the fabled Jim Bridger, the premier mountain man. Kit Carson trapped and traded, sometimes employed by the large fur-trading companies, such as Hudson's Bay Company, sometimes organizing his own enterprises. His reputation as an Indian fighter also increased. He led several expeditions against groups of Indians which had attacked trading posts or stolen horses from groups of trappers. As usual, he learned their languages and they, in turn, learned to trust this serious little man.

Sometime in 1838 Kit Carson met a Cheyenne maiden named Rai-Du, or Mountain Flower, and fell in love with her. Eventually they were married, and they spent a happy winter together at Bent's Fort in Colorado in 1839–40. After that winter, Kit Carson was always welcome to smoke the pipe of friendship in the lodges of the Cheyenne, Comanche, and Kiowa, but his brief period of domestic bliss ended tragically in late 1840 when Rai-Du died, following the birth of a daughter.

The welfare of the motherless infant was a constant worry to Kit. Finally, in the spring of 1842, he made temporary arrangements for her care and went to Missouri, hoping to find a permanent home for her there. His first visit to the Howard County homestead in seventeen years was in itself a tragedy. He found both his parents long dead and the farm in ruins. None of his brothers had stayed in Howard County, but Kit was able to trace his brother Robert to the fast-growing mecca of St. Louis, where Robert had a responsible position with one of the steamship companies which were prospering in trade along the Mississippi. Robert was happy to be reunited with his now-famous brother and readily agreed to provide a home for his motherless niece. Then he made arrangements for Kit to travel westward on a steamer going up the Missouri, perhaps the most important thing that ever happened to Kit Carson.

On the steamer he met John C. Frémont, who held a commission as a lieutenant in the United States Army Corps of Engineers. Despite this modest status, Frémont had acquired a reputation as an excellent mathematician and surveyor, but had not yet won fame as the surveyor and mapmaker of the routes to the far western frontiers. As the steamship moved up the Missouri, Frémont told Carson that he had been ordered to map a route to the mouth of the Columbia River on the Pacific Ocean. The task was difficult and had been made even more so when the guide he had hired failed to show up in St. Louis at the appointed time. It seemed natural for Carson the frontiersman to team up with Frémont the surveyor. Kit was hired as a guide at $100 a month.

The initial expedition started from northwestern Kansas early in June 1842. When they reached Fort Laramie, in Wyoming, the traders there warned them against going any farther that summer because of expected trouble with the Sioux. Kit advised Frémont that the Sioux could go on threatening trouble indefinitely. The situation could very well be worse next year, and there would be risks involved no matter how long Frémont waited. Frémont did not wait.

They set off through the Wind River mountain chain of the Rockies, surveying and sketching as they went. Kit's knowledge of the country and his ability to find paths over difficult terrain saved the party many days of hard climbing. Early in August they reached the South Pass, the crossing of the Great Divide. After Frémont and his chief assistant had made the necessary observations, the party turned back toward Fort Laramie, arriving early in September. Frémont and Carson parted company with no definite arrangement for carrying out the second stage of the mapping.

Kit was rehired by his former employers at Bent's Fort, not as a hunter this time, but as their representative at Taos. Kit had long since begun to consider Taos his home, so the assignment was most welcome. His happiness was compounded when he met Maria Josefa Jaramillo, a lovely young lady from an aristocratic Mexican family. Kit probably paid more attention to courtship that winter than he did to business, but he won the lady's hand. They were married in February 1843, with both the American and Mexican members of the community joining the celebration. Now Kit had a real home for his daughter. She was brought from St. Louis as soon as the trails were passable.

Early in June, Kit started for Bent's Fort, leaving his bride in Taos. On his arrival he was informed that Frémont had been there three days earlier to find out whether Kit could join him on a new expedition. Kit assembled his equipment, wrote a hurried note of explanation to his wife, and set off to catch up with Frémont.

Kit overtook Frémont about seventy miles from Bent's Fort. He found that great changes had been made in the composition of the party since the previous expedition. There were more men, they had more equipment, and there was a cavalry escort of some forty soldiers, commanded by a major.

Frémont's report of his first expedition had been well

received, but this was not the sole reason for the additional support. There were two more serious reasons: the United States was on the verge of war with Mexico over Texas and the Mexican Territory; and there was a serious debate going on with Great Britain over the Northwest Territories. The hot-heads among the American politicians were rallying to the cry of "Fifty-four-forty or fight!" They threatened to go to war to gain permanent control over all the territory south of latitude 54° 40′. It was hoped that the results of Frémont's surveying and mapping would strengthen the United States' claim to these territories, and he had been given plenty of money for expenses and for any special equipment he might need to speed up the expedition. He had been sent off from Washington like a conquering hero.

This time Frémont did not need to cross the Rockies in Wyoming, so he had Kit lead the party in a northwesterly direction, touching the eastern edge of the Great Salt Lake, then following the Bear River to Fort Hall, near the present city of Pocatello, Idaho. From there, Kit led them along the course of the Snake River to its junction with the Columbia and then on to the sea. A brief trip northward to a Canadian trading post on Vancouver Island and an equally fast trip back to the mouth of the Columbia completed all the specified goals of the expedition. The trip had been uneventful, and the United States now had a far better claim to the previously unexplored territory. But Frémont was not content. He decided to strike southward through Oregon into northern California.

The going was easy as far south as Klamath Lake. Game was plentiful, and the surveyors made copious notes about the lush country. Once past the lake, however, the land was less bountiful. Game became scarce and the party was forced to start using their supply of dried meat. Then, as if to test their determination, the snow-capped peaks of the Klamath Mountains blocked their path to the south, and the fourteen-thousand-foot volcanic cone of Mount Shasta towered ahead of them like a single massive sentry.

Kit and Frémont conferred. Neither of them had been over the mountains, but Kit had been in the Sacramento Valley, which they knew lay beyond. But how far beyond? Kit's estimate of 150 miles was very close. If they could have traveled in a straight line the distance would probably have been closer to ninety miles, but Kit had had enough experience to know that it is necessary to follow the path of least resistance when moving over rough country. They would have to wind through the valleys and along the ridges and go directly over mountains only when there was no other path open to them.

Frémont had to choose between a rough trip over the mountains into the lush Sacramento Valley or a return northward to Oregon. He chose to push on to California.

It is doubtful whether Frémont would have survived the trip through the mountains without Kit Carson, the mountain man. Moving ahead of the party, Kit found snowdrifts six feet or more deep. He returned to the floundering men and showed them how to fashion snowshoes from the branches of trees and brush, but this was no help for the horses and mules, which sank belly deep in every patch of soft snow. With Kit in the lead again, Frémont and his men slowly and painfully packed down a path for the animals to walk on. When the sun shone, the snow would melt a little and then freeze into a treacherous glaze when the sun's warmth disappeared. They were forced to scramble along the mountainsides, which were steep and slippery with snow and ice.

At the end of the twelfth day in the mountains, everyone but Carson was exhausted. Half of the animals were dead. It is probable that only Kit Carson's boundless energy and confidence kept them going. At sunset on that day he had returned to camp to announce that the Sacramento Valley was in view from the next ridge. Three days later they were out of the mountains. Kit shot some game, and then he and the six strongest men moved on to Sutter's Fort on March 6, 1844. Not a man had been lost during the entire ordeal.

Like any good surveyor or explorer, Frémont kept a detailed diary of the expedition. The notes from that diary were later converted into his official *Report of the Exploring Expedition to the Rocky Mountains, 1842, and to Oregon and North California, 1843–44,* which was released by the War Department in answer to the public clamor for details on this spectacular adventure. The report was widely quoted in the press and Frémont's generous praise of his chief scout, Kit Carson, gave new depth and luster to the public regard for an already famous frontiersman. One of the last incidents described in the report concerns an attempt by Carson and the expedition's chief hunter, Richard Godey, to rescue a group of Mexicans captured by raiding Indians.

Kit had led the party south through the central valley of California, through the Tejon Pass between the Sierra Nevada and Coastal ranges, and then eastward across the desert. Soon after they crossed the Colorado River, they encountered a Mexican man and a young boy who were the only remaining members of a trading party which had been attacked by Indians. The raiders had galloped off with all the livestock and equipment of the trading party and with all the survivors except these two. The captives included the man's wife and the boy's parents. As far as the man could tell, there had been about thirty braves in the party.

Kit immediately volunteered to track the raiders down and to try to free the captives. Godey also wanted to go along. They set out early in the afternoon and quickly found a faint but usable trail made by the fleeing Indians. When the early evening shadows made the trail impossible to follow, they rested for a while, then started again under the light of a full moon, riding until they were too tired to continue. They found a sheltered ravine and built a small fire that could not be seen from any distance. They huddled close to it, Indian-fashion, and got their sleep.

The wisdom of building a sheltered fire was proved shortly after they resumed the trail at daybreak. They were practically on top of the Indian camp. The Mexican had been correct. There were thirty braves wrapped in their blankets, still fast asleep. The livestock and other gear stolen from the traders were in plain view, but there were no signs of any captives. Kit felt sure they had already been killed, but he was determined to take back the livestock and to inflict some measure of punishment on the raiders. He and Godey tethered their horses in a grove of trees and began working their way toward the livestock.

Suddenly the animals sensed the presence of the two creeping men and began to stir. An Indian jumped up from his blanket, saw Kit and Godey, and began to shout the alarm. Kit's bullet struck him between the eyes. Godey fired at a second Indian, but missed. The two-man punitive expedition, with both their rifles empty, stood momentarily defenseless in the midst of the twenty-nine remaining Indians who were now firing arrows in swarms. Fortunately, excitement spoiled their accuracy. Reloading rapidly, Carson and Godey took aim and the Indians broke and ran. The rifles crashed out again and this time both bullets went home. With no compunction Carson and Godey scalped the three dead Indians.

Kit and Godey searched the deserted camp and found the grisly evidence they had expected. All the captives were dead. The two men gathered the livestock and headed back toward Frémont. The Frémont report concludes its description of the incident:

> Their objective accomplished, our men gathered up all
> the surviving horses, fifteen in number, returned upon their

trail, and rejoined us at our camp on the afternoon of the same day. They had rode about one hundred miles in the pursuit and return, and all in less than thirty hours. The time, place, object, and numbers considered, this expedition of Carson and Godey may be considered among the boldest and most disinterested which the annals of western adventure, so full of daring deeds, can present. Two men, in a savage desert, pursue day and night an unknown body of Indians into the defiles of an unknown mountain—attack them on sight, without counting numbers—and defeat them in an instant—and for what? To punish the robbers of the desert, and to avenge the wrongs of Mexicans whom they did not know. I repeat: it was Carson and Godey who did this . . . both trained to western enterprise from early life.

Kit Carson returned to his family early in July 1844, apparently determined to give up his roaming existence and settle down to farming. He and a friend, another mountain man named Richard Owens, bought land on the Cimarron River, about forty-five miles outside of Taos, and began building their homes. The houses were not even finished in June 1845 when a letter came from Frémont, who had recently been promoted to captain, urging Kit and any other qualified persons he could recruit to join him on a third expedition. Despite his wife's obvious disappointment, and the fact that she was expecting a child at any moment, Kit could not resist the call to adventure. He sold the land and the unfinished buildings for less than half of their worth, persuaded Owens to go with him, and rode off to meet Frémont at Bent's Fort.

This time Frémont had something truly different in mind. He wanted to explore the possibility of crossing over the mountains into California by going directly west from the Great Salt Lake, instead of heading northwest into Oregon. What made this plan startling was the fact that the land due west from the Salt Lake was a vast desert, held in awe by the

Indians who had inhabited the region for centuries. They believed that there was no water to drink, no game to hunt, and no grass to feed pack animals until the mountains on the far side were reached.

Frémont and Kit worked out a plan to find a route across this desert without endangering the entire expedition. Kit and three other mountain men, carrying an unusually large supply of water and food, would start across the desert, scouting the route and looking for water holes. If they found water they were to signal Frémont by building a smoky fire of pinecones. A second fire burning at the same time would tell Frémont that his scouts had also found game. Frémont would have observers scanning the desert with a telescope located at the top of a nearby mountain.

The four men made very good progress across the barren sand and rock. Kit was amazed at the range of temperatures they encountered, which were far greater than those he had experienced in the southern desert. The heat of the day was followed by cold so intense that they were forced to build a roaring fire when they stopped for the night. Early the next morning, after covering the fire with sand for fear it might make enough smoke to be seen by Frémont's lookout, they were on the move again, to make the most of the cool hours.

By noon on the second day they had reached the foothills of a small range of mountains near the present site of Wendover, Utah. They crossed what are now known as the Bonneville Salt Flats on their way. The crossing was unexpectedly easy, and they found water and grass to be plentiful among the small canyons of the foothills. They built a huge bonfire and heaped all their pinecones on it. The aromatic pine smoke billowed upward, rising undisturbed through the calm afternoon air. The sentry, about eighty miles away, spotted it and Frémont issued orders for the rest of the party to start at once.

The larger party did not make the crossing quite as quickly. It took them three days, during which several pack mules broke down under their loads. After rejoining Kit and his men, the party rested for two days and then pushed on to the west, having demonstrated that the feared desert could be mastered.

From this point on, each new day took them through territory that had never been seen by anyone but Indians. Hardly a day passed that the mapmakers did not record the location of an uncharted mountain or the course of a new river. Kit Carson rode out of camp early each morning to find the best route and then doubled back on his trail to meet the slower-moving caravan at the end of the day. In this way Kit traveled each day's route twice before Frémont and the bulk of the party ever saw it. By the light of the evening cook fires the scout would describe the next day's route to all the men. It was logical that many of the wonders they found were named for their discoverer—Carson River, Carson Lake, Lower Carson Lake, and the salt-rich Carson Sink.

It was winter by the time they reached the snowclad eastern slopes of the Sierra Nevadas, but the passage was not as difficult as the one they had made over the Klamath Mountains in 1844. This was largely because Kit discovered passes through mountains which permitted them to stay at lower altitudes and to avoid the ridge-running which had proved so difficult in crossing the Klamaths.

Using Sutter's Fort as a base, Frémont roamed over much of northern California during the spring and summer of 1846. During his wanderings he made a point of visiting all the American settlers in the area. But when Frémont attempted to ride to the flourishing port city of Monterey to buy supplies, Mexican officials decided they would not tolerate this band of armed Americans, led by an army officer,

approaching their headquarters. Frémont ignored their first
warning, but when the Mexicans sent a whole regiment of
troops after him, he decided to retreat to Klamath Lake in
Oregon. Here Frémont planned to rest his weary party for
several weeks before setting out again.

Their rest was almost immediately broken by the news
that the United States and Mexico had been at war since
May 13. Although his instructions from the War Department
had said nothing about taking part in any warlike activity,
Frémont immediately enrolled all the civilian members of
his party as militiamen, appointed Kit Carson an acting lieutenant, and set out for California and the Mexicans. For
some reason the Klamath Indians, who had not bothered the
party before, made repeated attacks on them as they made
their way back into the Sacramento Valley. Kit and his small
squad of scouts retaliated by raiding and destroying the
main Indian camp. Frémont suspected that the Mexicans
had set the Indians against him, but there was no proof.

The Mexicans far outnumbered Frémont's little band of
explorers but could never get them cornered. Both sides did
considerable maneuvering about the countryside but there
was no significant fighting. Finally a squadron of American
naval vessels sailed into the harbor at Monterey and forced
the Mexicans to flee. Frémont picked up a small force of
United States Marines from the naval squadron, recruited
more militiamen from among the American settlers, and
with his little army swollen to 150 men, marched southward.
Surprisingly, they were able to capture both Los Angeles
and San Diego.

Exultant over this unexpected success, Frémont asked
Kit to take a couple of his mountain men and carry dispatches back to New Mexico for relaying to Washington.
They set out in mid-September, assuming the role of trappers in case they encountered any Mexican troops. They

were, in fact, stopped several times, but their disguise held up. On October 6 Kit and his party met the main body of American troops marching across the Arizona desert to invade California.

Colonel Stephen W. Kearny commanded this reinforced regiment of about 1,700 troops. They had left Fort Leavenworth in June and had raised the American flag over Santa Fe in August. Kearny could not pass up the chance to acquire a scout as experienced as Kit Carson. He asked Kit to send the other men to Santa Fe with the dispatches and to return to California with him. Kit had been away from his family for more than a year and was at that moment hardly more than a few days ride from his wife and the infant daughter he had never seen. Nevertheless, he returned to California with Kearny.

The Mexicans had learned of Kearny's approach. They deployed a large force between the advancing American column and Kearny's goal—Frémont's base at San Diego. With Kit acting as the scout for his leading cavalry element, Kearny moved quickly to find the Mexicans and destroy them. Kit found the Mexicans easily enough and for two days the opposing forces marched and countermarched against each other without a decisive engagement. Kearny believed that they were too evenly matched. He asked Kit to try to get to Frémont in San Diego and bring back some reinforcements.

The Mexican army stood between them and San Diego, but this was an acceptable challenge to a man trained to make his way through hostile territory. Kit and his companion, Lieutenant Edward Beale, took off their boots and crept, crawled, and walked barefooted through the Mexican lines. Once clear of the Mexicans, they walked for two days and a night to reach San Diego. Frémont dispatched the reinforcements, but, ironically, Kearny was able to defeat the

Mexicans before the additional troops could arrive. The only significant battle in the campaign for California was over, but Kit Carson's exploits had made him the hero of the army.

As the senior American officer in California, Kearny took command of the growing American forces there. He and Frémont, who had now been promoted to brevet major, did not get along well. Frémont insisted that his original orders from the War Department authorized him to act independently, despite the fact that Kearny's orders, written a year and a half later, clearly gave Kearny command in California. The unfortunate dispute ultimately resulted in a court-martial for Frémont and a sentence of admonishment. When President Polk upheld the court-martial, Frémont angrily resigned from the army.

A man like Kit Carson, who was passionately loyal to his friends, could have easily become involved in the dispute, but by the fortunate happenstance of having been sent to Washington with dispatches, Kit was not present when the disagreement reached its peak.

Kit, in fact, had become the favorite of Washington society. Preceded by glowing dispatches from Kearny and already made famous by Frémont's report, Kit found himself lionized by the press and eagerly sought after as a dinner guest. He created a stir when he delivered his dispatches to the War Department clad in the dirty buckskins and moccasins he had worn on the trail.

Lieutenant Carson was sent back to California by way of New Mexico, where he had a brief reunion with his family before reporting to Kearny. After spending the winter of 1847–8 scouting for an attacking Mexican army that never arrived, he was again dispatched to Washington as a courier. While he was making that journey, the war with Mexico came to an end. Kit delivered his dispatches, collected several thousand dollars back pay, and set out for Taos.

Campaign dress of the American infantrymen, in 1847. This painting
shows a column of officers and enlisted men on the march

Kit Carson became a man of substance. His ranch prospered. He made good profits selling cattle and sheep to the hoards of gold seekers rushing across the country to answer the lure of California. Occasionally he participated in brief expeditions against unruly Indians.

In 1853 Kit was appointed Indian Agent for the New Mexico Territory. He took the job seriously, since he knew and respected the Indians and was sympathetic to their problems. His reputation for honesty and fair play served him well. No distance was too great for him to ride and no dispute was too petty to receive his attention. As the forces of the North and the South gathered for the great battles of the Civil War, Kit was enjoying most peaceful years.

When the Civil War finally erupted, Kit was appointed a lieutenant colonel in the First New Mexico Volunteer Infantry and later became its colonel. Although totally lacking in formal military education, Kit performed magnificently in operations against Confederate forces led by Brigadier General H. H. Sibley and later in action against the Indian tribes which chose this trying time to go on the warpath against federal forces they knew were weakened by the fighting in the East. Kit was made a brevet brigadier general on March 13, 1865, and was continued in active service after the Civil War ended because of his knowledge of the Indians. In October 1867 he and an aide rode out on an inspection tour. Something caused Kit's horse to shy, and he was thrown from the saddle. He never fully recovered from the resulting injuries, and he died the next year at the age of fifty-nine.

Pioneer, hunter, trapper, scout, soldier, explorer, rancher, businessman, protector of the peaceful Indian, and scourge of the warlike Indian—Kit Carson was a fabled hero in his own time and has been a model for Americans ever since.

5

J.E.B. Stuart
"Rides Around McClellan"

At West Point J.E.B. Stuart's classmates called him "Beauty," not so much to make fun of his homeliness as to pay tribute to his lively eyes and persuasive personality. Early in 1861, Stuart had been a captain in the First Cavalry Regiment, United States Army. Now, just fifteen months later, at the age of twenty-nine, he was a brigadier general in the Army of the Confederacy and was building a reputation for courage and showmanship.

On June 10, 1862, General Robert E. Lee summoned J.E.B. Stuart to his headquarters in Richmond, Virginia. As the young cavalry commander stood before Lee, the general noted that the undistinguished face was adorned with a flowing auburn beard and set off by a wide-brimmed cavalry hat with a long plume. Stuart's short, double-breasted cavalry jacket was encircled at the waist by a tasseled yellow sash, and his high black boots bore gold spurs. He was armed with a light French saber and a single pistol.

Standing in front of a map of the military situation in Virginia, General Lee described a scouting mission for Stuart's cavalry. Lee needed to know whether the Union forces under General George B. McClellan had begun to move westward from their bases along the Chickahominy River. As Lee and Stuart discussed the mission, the cavalryman began to conceive his plan for what was to be one of the most audacious reconnaissance operations in the history of warfare and one of the most famous actions in the Civil War.

As Stuart rode back to his camp on the outskirts of the city, he continued to think about his plan. He decided that if the federal troops had not moved westward in great strength from their base on the Chickahominy, he would be able to ride completely around McClellan's blue-clad army! He had mentioned the idea briefly to Lee, who had been impressed with its audacity, if not with its feasibility. The commanding general had not offered any encouragement, but at the same time he had not said "No."

The next day General Lee sent Stuart a letter order confirming their discussion. It read, in part:

> General,—You are desired to make a scouting movement to the rear of the enemy now posted on the Chickahominy, with a view of gaining intelligence of his operations, communications, etc., and of driving in his foraging parties securing such grain, cattle, etc., for ourselves as you can make arrangements to have driven. Another object is to destroy his wagon trains, said to be daily passing from the Piping-Tree Road to his camp on the Chickahominy. The utmost vigilance on your part will be necessary to prevent any surprises to your self, and the greatest caution must be practised in keeping well in your front and flanks reliable scouts to give you information. . . . Should you find, upon investigation, that the enemy is moving to his right, or is so strongly posted as to make your expedition inopportune, you will, after gaining all the information you can, resume your former position.

The balance of the long letter seems to have been directed at curbing Stuart's impetuosity. Lee cautioned the bearded cavalryman to keep his specific mission in mind, to avoid risking his command, and to be satisfied with doing as much as he could without feeling compelled to accomplish every secondary task. Knowing Stuart's preference for battle over pure scouting, Lee even felt it was necessary to reemphasize the primary mission of gaining intelligence.

Stuart proposed to make this scout with some twelve hundred men. With him would go Colonel Fitzhugh Lee and his First Virginia Cavalry, and Colonel W.H.F. "Rooney" Lee with the Ninth Virginia. Rooney was General Lee's second son and Fitz Lee's cousin. Stuart would split the Fourth Virginia between the cousins because its commander had been wounded and was not available for duty. He would also take the Jeff Davis Legion, an amalgamation of cavalrymen from Mississippi, Alabama, and Georgia and, as a final touch, two rifled cannon from the Stuart Horse Artillery.

The grand scale of the Stuart expedition reflected some of the changes that had taken place in warfare since the thirteen colonies cut themselves free from Great Britain. Many military historians, in fact, consider the Civil War the first truly modern war, because so many technical innovations were put into use. For the first time, railroads played an important part in a major war and messages were transmitted instantly by telegraph. Breech-loading and rifled cannon were common. Various kinds of repeating rifles and pistols found widespread use, and several rudimentary machine guns were tried out. When the Confederate navy sent ironclad wooden ships and a submarine into action, the Union navy responded with the first all-iron ships with gun turrets which could be rotated in any direction. The Union army also made widespread use of the first important advance in reconnaissance devices in many years—the observation balloon.

There is no record of Stuart's thoughts during the long hours of June 11, or of how he explained the fact that a courier from the commanding general had brought a message that was not made known to his staff. Knowing his character, it seems likely that the ebullient cavalryman must have wanted to shout his plans to the whole force, to let them know about the grand adventure they would embark upon very soon. But he kept his silence, sacrificing enthusiasm to secrecy. There were many Union spies around Richmond, and the success of his plan depended largely on secrecy and surprise.

At 2:00 A.M. on the morning of June 12, Stuart conducted his own kind of reveille, shaking his staff into consciousness and shouting cheerily, "Gentlemen, in ten minutes every man must be in the saddle!" No bugles blew but in an amazingly short time, twelve hundred men and two cannon had formed into a column and were moving out through the infantry pickets and northward along the Richmond, Fredericksburg, and Potomac Railroad.

The column moved twenty-two miles that day, harness jingling, horses snorting, and men behaving as though they were on some kind of carefree outing. Still there had been no word of their destination or purpose. The infantrymen they passed made pointed remarks about riding away from the fighting. Soon the rumor began to circulate that they were, in fact, on their way to reinforce General Stonewall Jackson in the valley of Virginia. Every mile northward strengthened the rumor.

The men and horses bedded down that night at the Winston Farm, close to the South Anna River. Stuart saw to the condition of his command and then rode with Rooney Lee to Hickory Hill, the family home of Rooney's wife. Lee spent a chatty evening with his in-laws while Stuart slept in his chair.

Before daylight on June 13, Stuart and Lee rode back to Winston Farm and another quiet reveille was conducted. The troopers expected to cross the river and continue to follow the railroad toward the north, and a murmur of wonder and anticipation ran down the mile-long column of horsemen when Stuart headed the column eastward. They were no longer skirting McClellan's army—they were headed directly toward it!

Stuart reined his horse off the road and sent a runner to assemble his field-grade officers. The time had come to tell the command just what they had been called upon to do. The enemy was close by, and Stuart could no longer afford any misunderstanding about their purpose. There would be no need for secrecy, anyway, once they had made their first contact with the bluecoats.

Stuart's scouts sighted the first Union soldiers near Hanover Courthouse at 9:00 A.M. and Fitz Lee was instructed to get his men behind the federal position. Unfortunately, Lee got his regiment bogged down in a marsh and the Union soldiers got away. Ironically, the Union soldiers were a scouting party from the Fifth Cavalry, Fitz Lee's old regiment.

The gray-clad cavalrymen trotted seven miles through the midday heat before seeing any more federal troops. Suddenly a small force of federal cavalry galloped out of the woods and bore down on the head of Rooney Lee's column. The bluecoats checked their plunge just short of the Confederates, fired a few shots, and raced away. Stuart quickly ordered a pursuit, but the federal patrol escaped unharmed. The best Stuart's men could do was to overrun a few outposts and capture a handful of dismounted federal cavalrymen. The prisoners were mostly old regular troopers from the Fifth Cavalry who immediately recognized Colonel Fitz Lee and greeted him. "Hello, Lieutenant!" they said, not knowing that he was now a colonel.

By this time Stuart was beginning to have misgivings about the enemy intentions. He was sure that the presence of his column had been reported far up the federal chain of command, and he expected to meet some sort of a defense at every road junction and stream crossing they passed. Finally the head of the Confederate column reached Totopotomoy Creek, a nasty little stream with a tangled maze of scrub trees overgrown with Virginia creeper along its banks. Stuart decided it was a logical place for a stout defense, and he sent half a squadron of cavalrymen across the stream on foot to explore the far bank. They found the same federal cavalry patrol that had retreated earlier, but after a token exchange of shots the federal patrol again galloped off to report the Confederate position.

A trooper of the Virginia cavalry

The lack of determined opposition by the Federals continued to bother Stuart, but he pressed forward down the road toward Old Church. He guessed that the next likely place for a Union defense was the point at which the road met the Mechanicsville Turnpike. This time he was right. The federal patrol that had been playing cat-and-mouse with Stuart's advance guard had reported the imminent arrival of the Ninth Virginia Cavalry to Captain Royall of the Fifth U.S. Cavalry. With two troops of the Fifth—about two hundred men—Captain Royall had prepared to defend the crossroad.

As Stuart approached the federal position, he could see that the Union cavalry was drawn up across the road and that the thick growth of trees on both sides left no room for any flanking movements. He therefore gave the orders for a headlong attack: "Form fours! Draw sabers! Charge!"

Captain Latane led the first Confederate troop that crashed into the Federals. Soon the narrow roadway was a melee of swinging sabers, smoking pistols, and screaming horses. Latane went down, shot dead. Royall was led away after suffering a saber slash from shoulder to elbow. The pressure from the Confederates was too great, so the Union cavalry began a series of quick withdrawals, followed by brief defenses.

Fitz Lee was sure the entire Fifth Cavalry was close at hand, and he begged Stuart's permission to go after them. Stuart consented, with the caution to Lee that the job must be done quickly. All Lee found, however, was the camp of the two cavalry troops they had just fought. He set the tents and wagons ablaze and "rescued" an ambulance wagon that carried a small keg of whiskey.

Stuart's primary mission had been fulfilled. He had discovered that there were no federal forces farther west than those originally reported to General Lee. McClellan had not extended his right flank. Now the commander of this over-size scouting force had to decide whether he should retrace his steps back to Richmond or continue ahead, passing entirely around McClellan's army.

There is little question that Stuart wanted to continue the encircling ride. He convinced himself that it was the correct course of action by accepting a series of assumptions. First, he assumed that the Federals would not leave the crossing over the Totopotomoy Creek unguarded a second time. Second, he assured himself that the Union troopers would be expecting him to retrace his steps and would be waiting for him at any one of a number of likely ambushes. The third assumption, and probably the least valid, was that the Union cavalry, under his own father-in-law, Brigadier General Philip St. George Cooke, would be rushing to cut off his retreat. Stuart should have known his wife's father better than that. The old soldier was the soul of caution. With the benefit of this hindsight, military historians will debate the validity of Stuart's reasoning as long as the Civil War is remembered.

But whether his reasoning was faulty or sound, Stuart had made up his mind—he would continue around McClellan. Before he gave the order to move on he summoned Lieutenant Mosby, one of his most trusted scouts, gave him two troopers as guides, and sent him ahead to scout the way.

With Mosby and his men about two miles ahead of the column, Stuart sent out a call for the men in his command whose homes were in the area and who knew the countryside well. These men were used to advise the regimental commanders of the local geography and were sent to seek information from civilians who lived close by. The local populace, who hadn't seen a gray uniform in several weeks, greeted them with a great deal of enthusiasm, but were unable to provide them with much useful intelligence about the Federals. The march continued with a series of false alarms and wild rumors but no contact with the Union army.

Stuart sent two squadrons eastward to Garlick's Landing to destroy some supplies that had been reported there, and turned the rest of the command more directly south, heading toward Tunstall's Station on the York River Railroad.

The road to Tunstall's gave mute evidence that their presence was well known. Abandoned wagons and deserted equipment dotted the roadside. The Union soldiers, whose job it had been to keep the outposts supplied, had left everything behind in their haste to get back to the safety of the main body of McClellan's army. Following the second part of Lee's instructions, Stuart made sure that everything of possible value to the Federals was destroyed. Many a Confederate trooper must have resented burning food that he would much rather have consumed himself. But the cavalry travels light, and Stuart could not consider gathering a train of supply wagons into his column.

The afternoon shadows were beginning to lengthen when the scouts brought word that Tunstall's Station was guarded by two companies of federal infantry. The troopers had been in the saddle constantly since sunup, but the news of impending combat brought them up in their saddles, ready for anything. When the head of the column was within sight of the station Stuart once again gave the command, "Form platoons! Draw sabers! Charge!"

The Union sentries, really just two squads totaling less than twenty men, were badly outnumbered. They broke and ran for the woods without making even a token defense. The delighted gray-clad troopers set to work, trying to break up the railroad tracks past the station and cutting down telegraph poles. Stuart knew that the destruction of this track would cut off all the Union forces along the Chickahominy from their supply base at the White House plantation,

Rooney Lee's family estate, which the Federals had captured. Axes were just beginning to bite into the railroad ties when the unmistakable sound of a train whistle was heard.

Hurried attempts were made to derail the train by throwing switches and by piling anything at hand on the tracks. The whistle sounded again, loud and long, a good sign to the Confederates that their presence at the station was not known. Troopers were ordered to set up ambushes on each side of the track, but many of them were still scrambling for cover when the train came within sight of the station. The train started to slow down as if to make a normal station stop, and some Federals riding on the string of flatcars hopped off the moving train. Suddenly an excited Confederate fired his pistol and the engineer released his brakes and applied full power. The rest of the Confederate cavalrymen opened up on the train with their pistols, inflicting many casualties on the federal troops who were huddled on the flatcars without any protection. The scout captain, Will Farley, grabbed a rifle, galloped after the engine, and shot at the engineer, but the train rolled faster and faster until it was out of sight. Stuart's remarks when he learned that his two cannon had got themselves stuck in a mudhole and were not available to blast holes in the engine as it went by are not recorded.

The escape of the train convinced Stuart that he could not achieve the ultimate glory of this great adventure—the destruction of McClellan's supplies at the White House plantation. Since the plantation was only four miles from Tunstall's Station, Stuart was forced to assume that the Federals knew where he was and that they would rush troops to the White House to defend it. Reluctantly, Stuart gave the command to move on, and the column headed southward toward St. Peter's Church and Talleysville.

Stuart's purpose now was simple—to get back across the

J.E.B. Stuart in full regalia, with his tasseled gold sash
and high leather boots

Chickahominy as quickly as possible. He started to head for the damaged but repairable Forge Bridge, but Lieutenant Jonas Christian, whose home was on the banks of the Chickahominy, advised him of a little-known ford at Sycamore Springs.

The road south from Tunstall's was in bad repair and it was slow going for the weary horses and riders. Some Confederates were now mounted on captured horses with the "U.S." brand on their flanks. A lot of captured mules with Union prisoners riding double on them ambled along with the gray-clad cavalry. At about 8:30 P.M., as the head of the column approached Talleysville, the exhausted artillery horses were just dragging their guns out of Tunstall's. The column that had left the Winston Farm that morning in sharp formation was straggling over three miles of road. The artillery pieces finally rattled into Talleysville at midnight.

Stuart ordered double teams on the cannon and made sure that every good horse or mule was carrying someone or something. The extra teams had hardly been harnessed into the guns when he gave the command to resume the march. He wanted very much to be across the Chickahominy by daylight.

Dawn was just making a fuzzy glow on the horizon when Lieutenant Christian led the advance element of the Ninth Virginia down the lane in Sycamore Springs and toward the ford. At the river's edge he drew up in shock and disappointment. The usually gentle Chickahominy was a black, roaring monster, swollen by heavy rains upstream. Rooney Lee, on one of the fresher horses, plunged into the flood and managed to make it to the far bank, but returned with the advice that the tired animals and men would be swept away if they tried to cross. Stuart stroked his beard as he tried to think of a way out of this predicament. He sent a reliable courier across the river with a message to General Lee telling him of the situation and asking that a demonstration be made by the nearest Confederate troops in the hope that this would tie down federal units which might otherwise be out chasing Stuart.

Then Stuart and his weary command set out for the Forge Bridge a mile farther downstream. They found only the abutments standing. With boards torn from a nearby warehouse and an old rowboat as a center support, the men built a shaky pontoon bridge that permitted a single trooper at a time to walk precariously across, carrying his saddle and leading his swimming horse by the reins. This process worked, but it was much too slow and the bridge would not support the weight of the artillery pieces. Finally the whole warehouse was battered down to yield its main timbers. Without knowing whether the timbers were really long enough to span the abutments, the tired men slowly and painfully dragged them to the edge of the near abutment and began to push them across. A cheer went up. They were just long enough! The guns could be saved!

The makeshift bridge was quickly floored and the column began to move across. Gradually the rear guard on the north side of the bridge was drawn in. The guns rolled across, then Fitz Lee pulled in the last of the rear guard, leaving five men behind to set fire to the timbers. Three valuable hours had been spent in bridge building. Now the flames crackled through the dry wood, and as the last of the Confederates loped away, a small group of federal cavalrymen raced up the road to the north side of the burning bridge and opened fire on the disappearing graycoats.

The ride around McClellan's army was over. Stuart, after turning the command over to Fitz Lee, made his way to General Lee. On the morning of June 15, just forty-eight hours after his cavalry had left the Winston Farm, Stuart returned to Lee's headquarters near Richmond. The slower-moving column did not reach the city until the sixteenth, when they received a welcome usually reserved for heroes. The people of the Confederacy took great pride in this new example of the superiority of the southern armies. In the North, Stuart's exploit again raised the doubts that had been plaguing both the public and the president. How could a force so small defy the entire Army of the Potomac? What was wrong with the Union generals?

Stuart's boundless ego absorbed the adulation like a sponge. A companion in the great adventure later commented to him, "That was a tight place at the river, General. If the enemy had come down on us, you would have been compelled to have surrendered."

"No," answered the hero of the ride around McClellan, "one other course was left."

"What was that?"

"To die game."

6

"Buffalo Bill" Cody, Paragon and Paradox

The story of Buffalo Bill is confounded by an almost impenetrable haze of imaginative memories, wishful thinking, and outright press-agentry. Through the mist that has clouded the story, some facts are clearly discernible but others are still obscure.

It is a fact that William Frederick Cody was born in Iowa in 1846. His place of birth was a real log cabin, which saved his promoters the trouble of providing an imaginary rustic birthplace. It is also a fact that his family migrated to the frontier in 1854, but they migrated southward to Kansas and not westward with the advancing pioneers. Their move to Kansas even lacked the hardships of real pioneering. The Cody family traveled in a carriage, while a hired man drove the wagon with their belongings. There were no nights out under the stars. Each day's travel was planned from county seat to county seat, and accommodations were arranged each night in a hotel or a private home.

Isaac Cody and his third wife, Mary, with eight-year-old William and the rest of their brood, were among the first legal settlers of the Kansas Territory. They established their homestead near Leavenworth, which at that time was the starting point for wagon trains taking the Oregon Trail westward. Young Billy seems to have led a quite normal country boyhood, which included learning to ride and shoot. But when his father died in 1857, he was faced with the necessity of supporting his mother and six sisters. Then Billy Cody told an untruth that was to follow him for the rest of his life. In applying for a job with a wagon-freighting company Billy said he had been born in 1845, and he was hired as a strong, intelligent, twelve-year-old. Actually, he was eleven.

The company had a contract to carry supplies to federal troops which had been sent to Utah to suppress the practice of the Mormon religion. Billy was signed on first as a herder of the extra horses, mules, and oxen, and then as a wagon driver. He made three trips to Utah, and on the last of these he killed his first Indian. The circumstances were not really heroic. The wagon train had been raided by Indians and all the stock had been driven off. The drivers, including Billy, set out on foot to get as far away from the Indians as possible. One night, when darkness fell, the tired boy found himself far behind his companions. As Billy approached the banks of the South Platte River, where the freighters had agreed to camp, a figure loomed up on the riverbank, silhouetted against the fading light. The sight of a war bonnet flowing from the head of this apparition brought an instinctive reaction from Billy. He raised his rifle and shot. The figure crumpled out of sight.

Then the boy realized that his shot might bring the Indian's companions. Billy crouched fearfully in the shadows, expecting to be attacked at any second. Nothing happened, however, and after waiting about half an hour, Billy left his hiding place and joined his companions. Back in Leavenworth, the tale of Billy's adventure grew with each telling, and the Cody legend was born. Buffalo Bill had killed his first Indian when he was only twelve! If his real age—eleven—had been known, the story would have been even better.

The broad plains were Billy's schoolroom and they taught him many valuable lessons, but they could not teach him the three R's. Once he returned from one of his wagon-driving adventures with almost a thousand dollars due in back pay. He proudly loaded his mother into a buggy to take her into Leavenworth to witness this big payoff. Mrs. Cody watched, horrified, as her son signed the payroll with an "x." As a result of motherly tears and admonishments, Billy agreed to go back to school and learn to write. He stayed at it long enough to learn to write his name and then set out on another adventure, scrawling "William F. Cody" on any surface that would accept a pencil mark.

By the time he was fourteen, young Billy had been introduced to buffalo hunting, had spent a year as a fur trapper, and had become one of the first Pony Express riders. These ventures took him as far west as Denver, as far north as the Canadian border, and as far south as the Oklahoma Territory. It is no wonder that he later proved to be an unerring scout during the Indian wars.

Billy Cody was the youngest of the eighty riders hired to man the new Pony Express in March 1860. Working in relays, the riders carried the mail from St. Joseph, Missouri, to Sacramento, California, in eight or nine days. Their routes carried them through some very rugged country and they were often exposed to attack by hostile Indians. If a relief rider were not available to carry the mail pouch on the next relay, company rules required the original rider to continue to the next relief point, exchange pouches with a relief rider there, and then return immediately to his starting point. On one such occasion Cody arrived at the end of his normal relay to find that the relief rider had been killed in a drunken brawl the night before. Billy Cody continued to the end of the next relay, then doubled back over the entire route. In a period of twenty-one hours and forty minutes he rode twenty-one horses and covered a distance of 322 miles.

The completion of the transcontinental telegraph brought a quick end to the Pony Express after it had been in operation for only a year and a half. The last ride was made on October 21, 1861, and then Billy Cody found himself unemployed.

The United States was being torn apart at this time on the slavery issue, and feelings ran high in Leavenworth, which was on the border between slave-holding Missouri and free Kansas. When the war between the states broke out, Billy supported the Union side and took part in the partisan fighting which characterized the early stages of the war in the border states. For two years he mixed into the operations of irregular cavalry companies which were hardly more than groups of uniformed horse thieves. Then on February 4, 1864, the Seventh Kansas Volunteer Cavalry Regiment rode into Leavenworth to spend thirty days' leave. When the regiment rode back to the war, Private Bill Cody rode with it.

There is some doubt about what Private Cody's duties with the Seventh Kansas were. Some of his biographers insist that he was primarily a scout. Others say that he was a scout only in the sense that he carried messages through dangerous territory. In his autobiography, written many years later, Cody says he was picked by Major General Andrew Jackson Smith to get out and find the elusive Nathan Bedford Forrest, who almost always seemed to "get there first with the most" men.

Traveling in disguise, which made him technically a spy rather than a scout, Cody adopted a Tennessee drawl and was able to move freely through the Confederate army. He recalled that on his way back, "I passed several detachments of Forrest's troops, but my training as a scout enabled me to keep them from seeing me."

One thing is certain about Cody's service during the Civil War: he never dodged a fight. In some way he took part in every action that the Seventh Kansas fought while he was a member. The most famous of these was the battle at Tupelo, Mississippi, on July 14, 1864, when General Smith actually caught up with Forrest and punished his army severely. Had Smith been a little more aggressive and pressed the advantage he gained in the first day's fighting, Forrest might have been eliminated as a threat to the advancing Union army.

When the war ended, all the volunteer regiments were mustered out of service, leaving the regular army with the task of maintaining law and order in the vast new western territories. Bill Cody had just been discharged from the Seventh Kansas when he first met General William Tecumseh Sherman, who had been sent west to negotiate a peace treaty with the Kiowa and Comanche Indians. Cody signed on to accompany Sherman's small party, not as a scout but as a messenger. Within a few days after their departure from Leavenworth, Cody had so impressed Sherman with his intimate knowledge of the country that the general changed the young man's status to that of scout. Cody promptly proved his skill by leading Sherman directly to the spring at which the Indians were camped, where the treaty was concluded with much ceremony. Sherman was thus able to return to Chicago, and Cody was once again unemployed.

Perhaps out of boredom, Cody traveled to St. Louis, Missouri, to court a lady he had met some time before. His courtship was successful and he returned to Leavenworth with a bride. The charming southern lady who had become Mrs. Cody never played an important part in his life. She detested frontier life from the outset, and when Billy proved unsuccessful at several speculative business ventures, she returned to St. Louis, where she received infrequent visits from her husband. These visits resulted, ultimately, in the birth of five children—four girls and a boy, Kit Carson Cody.

Bill Cody now hired himself out as a buffalo hunter for a company which had a contract to provide food for railroad construction crews of the Kansas Pacific Railroad. He was paid the handsome sum of $500 a month to compete with hostile Indians for twelve buffalo each day. This particular job lasted eight months, and he claimed to have delivered 4,280 buffalo carcasses to the construction crew tents. If this figure is correct, his daily bag would have been somewhat higher than the twelve he contracted to deliver, but since buffalo hunting was a sport in which he excelled, there is no reason to doubt the higher figure. By the time his contract expired he had been dubbed "Buffalo Bill."

Since "William" is a common name and since there were many buffalo hunters, there were several other claimants to the name of "Buffalo Bill." Legend has it that Bill Cody won undisputed possession of the name "Buffalo Bill" in a contest with Bill Comstock, another hunter. The two men agreed that the one who could kill the greatest number of buffalo in a single day would henceforth be the only real "Buffalo Bill." The contest took place twenty miles east of Sheridan, Kansas, with a large audience present to watch the slaughter, make side bets, and drink champagne. The match started at eight o'clock in the morning and ended at four in the afternoon. The score: Cody—69; Comstock—46. It is interesting to note that Cody's recollection of the exact site of the contest has been verified by an archeological discovery; not of heaps of buffalo bones, but of a considerable stack of hand-blown champagne bottles.

After the railroad job came to an end, Buffalo Bill was

again unemployed. In May 1868, he joined the scouts for the Third Infantry at Fort Larned. From this point on, the accuracy of army records begins to push back the haze of doubt about Cody's career. Although he had many detractors, particularly after he embarked on his theatrical enterprises, few of their charges of falsification or exaggeration about his service with the army were ever verified. In August 1868, he transferred to the Tenth Cavalry and one of its officers described the new scout:

> Bill Cody, one of our scouts and one of the best shots on the plains, keeps us well supplied with plenty of buffalo and deer. He gets $60 per month and a splendid mule to ride, and is one of the most contented and happy men I ever met.

Still untouched by fame, Bill Cody rode with the army dressed very much like any ordinary frontiersman of the time. He wore a coarse wool shirt, blue corduroy trousers stuffed into common calf-length boots, and a broad-brimmed felt hat. He carried a skinning knife on his belt and a cap-and-ball pistol in a holster. His primary weapon was still "Lucretia Borgia," a .50-caliber Springfield rifle that he had used to hunt buffalo. Cody stuck to this single-shot breech-loader because he knew that anything he hit with its huge slug would go down to stay. He was willing to sacrifice the rapid fire of the new repeating rifles for the sure kill of "Lucretia Borgia."

The late summer of 1868 brought an unexpected upsurge of Indian raids and attacks on white settlers. General Philip Sheridan had made an honest try to adhere to the treaty written at Medicine Lodge the previous fall, but with only 2,600 soldiers to police the area west of the Missouri and south of the Platte, he suddenly found the Cheyenne and the Sioux on the warpath. In answer to his request for more troops, seven companies of the Fifth United States Cavalry were hastily dispatched from posts in the former Confederate states and assembled at Fort Hays, Kansas. There they picked up the chief scout whom General Sheridan had personally selected—Bill Cody, of course. The relationship between the regiment and the scout lasted many years and brought Buffalo Bill his greatest fame.

The winter of 1868–9 was a particularly bitter one. General Sheridan hoped to campaign throughout the winter in order to take advantage of the hardship the cold brought to the Indians, so the Fifth Cavalry paused only briefly at Fort Hays before continuing westward to Fort Lyon in Colorado. Sheridan's plan of action called for the Fifth to deploy back toward the southeast, into Oklahoma, and to keep the Indians from moving toward the open spaces of the west. Sheridan himself, with Custer's Seventh Cavalry, some Kansas cavalry, and five companies of regular infantry, left Fort Larned to push into the Indian territory of western Oklahoma, forcing the Indians toward the Fifth Cavalry. At the same time, Sheridan ordered six troops of the Third Cavalry and two companies of infantry to move northeastward out of New Mexico to block the Indians' escape to the south.

During that hard winter Cody lived up to his reputation of knowing the country better than any other scout. His experience as a wagon driver proved invaluable, since the Fifth Cavalry always traveled with its complete wagon train, contrary to the common practice of cavalry traveling light and returning frequently to a fort for provisions. Cody found water when even Indian scouts working with the regiment could not, and his skill with "Lucretia Borgia" provided fresh buffalo and antelope when scurvy began to break out among the troops. Actually, the Fifth saw little fighting that winter and Cody was miles away from the single small engagement that took place.

The Fifth returned to Fort Lyon in February 1869. The fighting was over for a while. The Kiowas and Comanches had started to negotiate for a new peace treaty right after they were beaten by Custer and the Seventh Cavalry in a battle along the Washita River. The Cheyennes held out until March 1869, when Custer forced them to make peace.

Cody's performance that winter was rewarded in an unusual, if gratifying, way. Brevet Major General Eugene Carr, senior officer of the Fifth and its commander during the winter campaign, directed the regimental quartermaster to pay Cody what was due him at his contract salary of $75 per month, discharge him, then rehire him at $125 per month, retroactive to the previous October! With this unexpected windfall in his pocket, Cody set off for St. Louis to visit his wife and daughter.

Buffalo Bill apparently showed up at Fort Lyon later that spring wearing the outfit in which he is most frequently pictured. Carr describes his scout as being decked out in fringed buckskins, instead of the old woolen shirt and corduroy pants. Cody had also let his hair grow during the winter and he made a picturesque sight with his long, wavy hair falling from the shadow of a broad-brimmed white hat. His grand appearance did not help much when he signed on with the regimental quartermaster. Congress had been hard on the army during the winter and Buffalo Bill went back on the payroll at only $75 per month.

The regiment left Fort Lyon on May 1 and began to work its way northeastward by a roundabout route to Cheyenne Wells and Fort Wallace in Colorado. On May 13 Cody discovered unmistakable signs of a large group of Indians and galloped back to the column to report to General Carr. The commander immediately sent Cody back to confirm his find, but provided an escort of twelve troopers with a lieutenant in charge. Following the course of a creek to about five miles downstream from his point of first discovery, Cody and the lieutenant dismounted and crawled to the top of a knoll. From this vantage point they could see an Indian village some three miles farther downstream. A messenger was sent back to Carr, but on the way he was discovered by some roving Indians and chased back to the protection of Cody's patrol. While the soldiers set out to drive the Indians away, Cody rode back and made his report to Carr.

Five companies were immediately organized and guided back toward the Indian camp by Cody. In the meantime, the Indians, knowing they had been discovered, had broken camp and started the women and children moving north toward the Republican River. The braves then set up an ambush which succeeded in trapping Company B of the advancing cavalry. The company was rescued after it had lost four men and had killed thirty Indians. The Indian war party made an expert withdrawal under the cover of darkness.

With an advance guard of forty men and two officers, Cody followed the trail of the warriors for three days— right into another ambush! Two hundred Indians attacked the advance guard and surrounded it. In classic cavalry fashion the troopers formed a circle, dismounted, and fired at the Indians with one hand, holding their horses with the other. In this fashion the circle was "walked" back toward the main column, some three miles away.

The Indians fought desperately in order to cover the withdrawal of their women and children, and as his supplies were running low, General Carr was willing to break off. He let the surviving Indians cross the Republican and then led his troops north to Fort McPherson. In his official report Carr heaped praise on Cody's ability as a scout, a fighter, and a marksman. The unique part of the report, however, was a recommendation that Cody receive an extra $100 for his "extraordinarily good services." Since this was a most unorthodox manner of rewarding someone, the request had to go all the way to the secretary of war for approval. No other scout had ever been rewarded in this fashion.

The Fifth Cavalry moved out of Fort McPherson on June 9, 1869, to search for a large band of Dog Soldiers led by Tall Bull, a Cheyenne. The Dog Soldiers were members of an Indian warrior sect which included Cheyennes, some Arapahos—the traditional allies of the Cheyenne—and some Sioux. Although many whites considered them to be nothing more than renegades, the Dog Soldiers were respected by the tribes that had made peace with the white men. It seems that Indian custom permitted any member of a tribe who did not personally take part in a tribal agreement to behave as though there were no agreement at all. Thus the Dog Soldiers could continue to fight the whites and still remain in the good graces of their tribes. Tall Bull had exercised this freedom of action while the Fifth Cavalry was preparing itself at Fort McPherson. His band had raided settlers along the Solomon River and had carried off two white women. The first objective of the Fifth's summer campaign in 1869 was to rescue these women.

Three companies of Pawnee Indian scouts, led by white officers, joined General Carr's forces to assist with the scouting. Although Indian scouts had been in use for some time, the practice of forming them into units capable of light combat was relatively new. Their officers were usually not regulars but frontiersmen who had been commissioned in a state militia and then hired by the army to form the Indian units and lead them. The three companies with the Fifth Cavalry had been formed by Major Frank North. There was no love lost between the Pawnees and the Cheyennes, so the Indian scouts saw nothing wrong in joining the white soldiers in the search for Cheyenne scalps.

By July 8 the cavalry had picked up Tall Bull's trail, and

finding the marks of women's soled shoes around several cold campfires, had confirmed that the two white women were still held prisoner. Apparently unaware that he was being followed, Tall Bull set a leisurely pace northward toward the Black Hills of Wyoming and the Powder River country. On July 10 General Carr ordered his troops to make camp for the night on a campsite that the Indians had vacated that morning. Now the Dog Soldiers were only a day ahead of their pursuers.

Carr decided to leave his wagon train and all troopers with unfit horses where they were while he took the remaining 240 officers and men and 50 Pawnee scouts to close in on Tall Bull. They moved out of camp at two o'clock in the morning on July 11. By mid-morning Cody had discovered Tall Bull's pony herd grazing peacefully under the dozing care of a fifteen-year-old Indian boy. After reporting this to Carr, Cody was again sent out, this time with a small group of the best Pawnee scouts, to find the main Indian village. They located it at about noon and Cody left the Pawnees to keep watch while he went back to make his report.

Although Cody had not seen any Indian sentries, he assumed that Tall Bull would surely have posted lookouts back along the trail they had followed from the south. For this reason he recommended to Carr that the troops make a wide swing around the village and attack from the north. Carr accepted this suggestion, even though it would cause a delay in the final attack. It was 1:30 in the afternoon before the Fifth Cavalry was in position. As the sharp notes of the bugle sounded "Charge!" the troopers galloped across the open prairie straight into the Indian camp.

The surprised Dog Soldiers fought fiercely, but they were at a great disadvantage without their horses. Many of the warriors managed simply to slip away in the confusion. Bill Cody, always on the lookout for a good horse, told this tale:

I was on the skirmish line, and noticed an Indian who was riding a large bay horse, and giving orders to his men in his own language.

I could understand part of what he said. He was telling them that they had lost everything and were ruined, and was entreating them to follow him until they died. The horse this chief was riding was extremely fleet. I determined to capture him if possible, but I was afraid to fire at the rider lest I kill the horse.

Often the Indian, as he rode around the skirmish line, passed the head of a ravine. It occurred to me that if I dismounted and crept up the ravine, I could, as he passed, easily drop him from the saddle with no fear of hurting the horse. Accordingly I crept into the ravine and secreted myself there to wait till Mr. Chief came riding by.

When he was not more than thirty yards away I fired. The next instant he tumbled from the saddle and the horse . . . galloped toward the soldiers, by one of whom he was caught.

Bill Cody had killed Tall Bull.

As a result of this action, one of the white women was rescued (an Indian squaw had killed the second white woman with a tomahawk), more than 50 Dog Soldiers were killed, and 270 horses were captured. One member of the Fifth Cavalry was scratched by an arrow.

Bill Cody had guided the regiment along the Indian trail. He had found the Indian camp and had recommended a successful route of attack, but only the official army reports mentioned his scouting contribution. To the public, Buffalo Bill Cody became the man who had killed Tall Bull in glorious mortal combat. A new phase of life was beginning.

Less than a month and a half after the battle with Tall Bull and his Dog Soldiers, Bill Cody met the man who gave him his first taste of national publicity. This was Ned Buntline, a deserter from the Union army during the Civil War, an occasional temperance lecturer, and a sometime writer of dime novels. "Ned Buntline" was a pseudonym, of course, but his pen name became famous while his real one was practically unknown. In any case, Cody and Buntline met on a Union Pacific train. Cody was with a troop of the Fifth Cavalry moving by rail to pursue some Indians who had just raided an isolated railroad station. Buntline was on his way east after an unsuccessful temperance lecture tour in California.

Buntline accompanied the cavalrymen on their Indian hunt and impressed Cody with his horsemanship. When the troops returned to their home station, Buntline apparently continued his trip eastward, for the December 23, 1869, edition of the *New York Weekly* carried the first installment of *Buffalo Bill, The King of the Border Men.*

For some reason, Buntline chose to overlook the battle with Tall Bull and the Dog Soldiers and instead wrote a completely fanciful yarn about young Cody as a semimilitary raider during the Kansas-Missouri actions early in the Civil War. Buffalo Bill, still the trusting, unaffected frontiersman, was delighted with the stories, even if they were pure fiction. When the Codys' first son was born, Buffalo Bill wished to name him after Buntline, but wiser heads prevailed and the unsuspecting infant was modestly named Kit Carson Cody.

For the next six years Buffalo Bill Cody the scout was almost completely submerged by Buffalo Bill the showman. General Sheridan began the practice of bringing rich sportsmen from Chicago to Fort McPherson for buffalo hunting with the man known as the best buffalo hunter in the world —Buffalo Bill. When these men returned to the East, they spread the word of Cody's skill and daring. Cody began playing the part. His buckskins were now white, and the open leather jacket revealed a red silk shirt. When greeting new arrivals to these hunting expeditions, he left his faithful hunting horses in the stable and galloped up on a white horse, waving his white sombrero in welcome.

The summer of 1876 became the most famous period in the history of the Indian wars. The fighting, which had become scattered and less frequent, suddenly flared up to a scale never before experienced.

An ill-advised order, issued by the Interior Department through the Indian commissioner, directed tribes and families, known as "lodges" by the Indians, to move back onto their reservations in the dead of winter. Instead of complying with the order, 40 lodges under Sitting Bull and 120 lodges led by Crazy Horse of the Ogallala Sioux united and faced the army with an enemy force that could muster several thousand warriors at any given time.

The deadline for compliance with the order to move back onto the reservations was January 31, 1876. When none of the lodges showed any sign of obeying the order, General Sheridan began mapping one of his typical encircling operations to hold the Indians in place south of the Missouri River, north of the Niobrara, and away from the frontier settlements. General Crook, with three regiments, was dispatched to the north from Fort Fetterman, Wyoming. Colonel John Gibbon moved east from Fort Ellis, Montana, with the Seventh Infantry. The Seventh Cavalry moved to the west from Fort Abraham Lincoln, near Bismarck, North Dakota, under the command of Brevet Major General Alfred Terry. The regiment's assigned commander, Brevet Major General George Armstrong Custer, was in Washington and could not rejoin his troops for several weeks.

In the meantime, the Fifth Cavalry was called back from Arizona and assembled at Cheyenne, Wyoming. It was instructed to scout the territory between the advancing columns of Terry and Crook. The regiment was ready to go into action early in May 1876, but it lacked its favorite chief scout. Several letters were written to Bill Cody, who was on tour in the East with a theatrical company. It took six weeks for Cody to make his decision, which was complicated by his obligations to the theater company and by the recent death of young Kit Carson Cody. But by June 10 the name of William F. Cody was once again scrawled on the payroll of the Fifth Cavalry.

Old hands in the regiment recalled that Cody looked pretty much as he had when they had last seen him in '69, except that he seemed "a little worn, probably caused by his vocation in the east not agreeing with him." The oldtimers also drew confidence in seeing General Carr and Cody together again. With such a leader and a scout, they were sure, they "could get away with all the Sitting Bulls and Crazy Horses in the Sioux Tribe."

The regiment moved to Fort Laramie on June 11 and then started northward into the Red Cloud Indian Reservation, or Agency, on June 22. On July 1, Brevet Major General Wesley Merritt, the new colonel of the Fifth Cavalry, joined his command and General Carr stepped down to become a squadron commander. On July 7 an official dispatch notified General Merritt that Custer and five companies of the Seventh Cavalry had been wiped out at the Little Big Horn on June 25.

On July 11 the Fifth Cavalry was ordered to retrace its steps southward to Fort Laramie to join Crook. On the fourteenth, information was received from the Red Cloud Agency that more than a thousand Cheyenne were about to leave the reservation. Since Merritt's initial orders had specifically instructed him to stop all Indian movement to the west, the regiment was again countermarched to the north to be in position to intercept the Cheyenne. The Fifth moved eighty-five miles in thirty-one hours to reach the trail the Cheyenne were to take. Outposts and signal stations

were set up at once and Bill Cody set out by himself to find
the Indians. As dawn began to break on the morning of July
17, Cody galloped up to General Merritt's tent and reported
that a large group of Indians was breaking camp not far
down the trail and had already begun to send scouts toward
the cavalry's position. Cody had hardly delivered his message when Lieutenant King of Company K signaled that
Indians were in sight.

Generals Merritt and Carr, with a few staff officers and a
half-dozen troopers, rode to Lieutenant King's vantage point
and were joined there by Cody and two other scouts. A
group of about forty Indians could be seen plainly, and it
was also plain that the Indians did not realize the cavalry
was near, since they made no effort to conceal themselves.

Suddenly the Indians became excited and began to point
back toward the south. They had discovered two troopers
riding hard toward the still-unseen cavalry. It later turned
out that the two soldiers had been carrying a message from
the main supply train, which had been left behind by the
rapid pace of the mounted troops. At that moment, however,
they were leading the Indians straight into the middle of the
Fifth Cavalry, down a draw that was directly in front of the
regimental commander and his staff.

What happened then is reported in several different
versions, most importantly those of Bill Cody and Lieutenant
King. Cody's version first:

> The commander asked me if I had any suggestions.
>
> "General," I replied, "why not wait until the scouts
> [the Indians] get a little nearer? When they are about to
> charge on the two men, I will take fifteen soldiers, dash
> down and cut them off from their main body. That will
> prevent them from going back to report, and the others
> will fall into our trap."
>
> The general at once saw the possibilities of the scheme.
> "If you can do that, Cody, go ahead," he said.

Cody then says he went back to the main camp and picked out fifteen of the best men he could find and got them into position to attack on General Merritt's order. Soon the order came: "Go on now Cody, and be quick about it. . . ." A brief but lively fight followed in which three Indians were killed, but several escaped. Suddenly the Indians who were riding away stopped and turned around for another charge. A second fight began, and in the midst of it, according to Cody:

> One of the Indians, who was elaborately decorated with all the ornaments usually worn by a great chief when he engaged in a fight, saw me and sang out:
> "I know you, Pa-ho-has-ka! Come and fight with me!"
> The name he used was one by which I had long been known by the Indians. It meant Long-Yellow Hair.
> The Chief was riding his horse to and fro in front of his men, in order to banter me. I concluded to accept his challenge . . .

And so they fought. Cody killed the Indian's horse with his first shot, then his own horse stepped in a hole and fell, leaving the two antagonists facing each other, not more than twenty feet apart. They both fired at the same instant, but Cody's luck held. The chief's bullet whizzed by Cody's ear and Cody's bullet struck the chief "full in the breast." The Indian had hardly hit the ground when Cody was on him to apply the *coup de grace* with a knife stroke to the heart.

And so Bill Cody killed sub-chief Yellow Hand (whose real name was also Yellow Hair) in a single mortal combat after accepting the Indian's taunts as a challenge to his honor.

How did Lieutenant King report this action? We start at the same point in time, with the messengers being chased down the draw toward Merritt, Carr, Cody, King, et al:

"By jove! General," said Cody, sliding down the hill toward his horse, "now's our chance. Let our party mount here out of sight, and we'll cut those fellows off."

"All of you keep out of sight," Merritt ordered. "Mount now, and when the word is given, off with you. Watch them, King. Give the word when you are ready."

According to King, Cody was given the honor of leading the group because he had thought of the idea. Cody's total command consisted of the other two scouts and five troopers of Company K.

In King's account, the combat between Cody's little force and the Indian scouts had hardly begun when a cry went up from other lookouts and the main band of Indian warriors appeared on a nearby ridge. General Merritt saw that the war party was riding hard to come to the assistance of the scouts, and he ordered the first full cavalry company forward to meet the charge. King recalled that, as he mounted his horse:

> ... I see Buffalo Bill closing in on a superbly accoutered warrior. It is the work of a minute; the Indian has fired and missed. Cody's bullet tears through the rider's leg, into his pony's heart, and they tumble in a confused heap on the prairie. The Cheyenne struggles to his feet for another shot, but Cody's second bullet crashes through his brain, and the young chief, Yellow Hand, drops lifeless in his tracks.

The result is the same. Cody kills Yellow Hand in both versions, but his own version was written after many years of re-creating a dramatic version of the "Duel with Yellow Hand" for theater and Wild West shows. King wrote his description of the fight within four years of the event, and he had the initial advantage of watching the "duel" instead of fighting it. Official records which contain descriptions by other members of the Fifth Cavalry, none of them as complete as either Cody's or King's, verify the accuracy of King's memory. The "Duel with Yellow Hand" stands as one of the most interesting comparisons of fact versus the Cody legend.

Buffalo Bill never fought a major battle again. He returned to the stage in the fall of 1876 to produce an extravaganza centered on Custer and the Yellow Hand episode. From time to time Cody did return to the frontier in what he claimed to be honest efforts to help with the Indian problem, but to the public, his efforts always had the taint of publicity-seeking.

Despite this taint, William F. Cody was a fine example of all the things a scout must be. That he ended his days as a well-to-do showman instead of a penniless buffalo hunter is a tribute to his good sense rather than a criticism of his abilities.

Let the final accolade come from Lieutenant King, who later became a novelist as well as a general:

> He was a beautiful horseman, an unrivalled shot, and as a scout unequalled. We had tried them all . . . They were all noted men in their way, but Bill Cody was the paragon.

"Buffalo Bill" Cody with former enemies at Pine Ridge, South Dakota, where, on January 16, 1891, a final peace was made with the Sioux Nation

7

The Indian Scouts

Chincachgook and his son Uncas, characters in James Fenimore Cooper's *The Last of the Mohicans,* have taken their places in American literary history as the most famous Indian scouts. They typify the idealized Indian scout who glides noiselessly through the woods, a shadow among the shadows, reading the meaning of every broken twig and every footprint, his every sense straining to the task of finding his quarry. It made little difference whether the quarry was a deer or an enemy war party; the search was conducted in very much the same way for either.

To some degree, all Indian warriors were scouts. They were trained in the skills of tracking and observation from boyhood. As they grew older, they were schooled in the use of weapons for both hunting and fighting. They learned the intricate secrets of nature in their tribal homeland, whether that home was in the deep forests of the Adirondacks, on the plains and rolling hills of the Dakotas, or on the rocks and sand of Arizona. The Indian hunter-warrior-scout was a product of his particular environment, and as long as he remained in that environment, few enemies could get the better of him. Summing up years of experience in fighting

Indians, Colonel John Gibbon of the Seventh Infantry wrote in 1877:

> To the Indian, every foot of the country he is operating in is as familiar as are the paths of our flower gardens to us. He has traveled and hunted over it since childhood, knows every path, every pass in the mountains and every water-hole as thoroughly as the antelope or other wild animals which range through it. He knows exactly where he can go and where he cannot, where the troops can come and will come, and where they cannot, and he knows the points from which he can safely watch the whole country, and give timely notice of the movements of troops, and direct those of his own camps so as to avoid an encounter, or concentrate to meet one.

A few white men learned these skills and turned them into tools for the successful exploration of the Indian country. Daniel Boone was probably the most noteworthy of the men who were not essentially military scouts but who used the scouting and woodsman's skills to safeguard themselves and their parties while exploring.

Other white men sincerely took the Indians' skills unto themselves, nurtured them, and sometimes even improved upon them. But even these men usually reached a point in their lives when their attachment to nature and to the scout's craft was subdued by the desire to live like other white men. Kit Carson, who probably had more real knowledge about the Indian and genuine sympathy for his problems than any of his white contemporaries, ended his days in civilized comfort and comparative wealth. Scouting was a basic part of the Indian's way of life. To the white man it was merely a device, a means to an end that could be cast aside and forgotten when that end was achieved.

The first white settlers in America quickly learned that they could put the Indians' scouting skills to good use. The

French explorers of the St. Lawrence River and the Mississippi basin used Indians to guide them and to supply food for the exploring parties. When France and England went to war over possession of North America, they both found, or bought, Indian allies. The worst depredations of the French and Indian War were committed by Indian scouting or raiding parties attached to regular military forces.

In his campaign against the rebellious Americans in 1777, British General Burgoyne made good use of a large number of Mohawk Indians. While they were with him, scouting and conducting harassing raids on the retreating Americans, Burgoyne had little difficulty in out-maneuvering the American General Horatio Gates. But Burgoyne contributed to his own downfall by insisting that his Indians spare women and children found during raids. On one occasion, when an Indian party killed a white woman, Burgoyne punished them so severely that they simply walked away from his army. They could not understand the white man's ways.

The Indians defended their tribal homes against the advance of the white settlers, but slowly, steadily, the frontier fringe of settlements expanded in ever-widening circles. There were too many white men with too many guns. The Indians' fighting skill and knowledge of their homeland were their best defensive assets, and they used them well. As the white men drove the Cherokee from Georgia and South Carolina, the Creek from Alabama, the Delaware from Pennsylvania, and the Seminole from Florida, the Indians made the whites pay a high price for their conquest. There was bloody fighting with little attention paid by either side to the rules of formal warfare.

Some of the defeated tribes were moved westward to less valuable land, selected for them by solicitous white men. Others, such as the Iroquois nation and the Mohicans, were so exhausted by years of constant fighting and by the inroads of disease that they were permitted to stay in their homelands. By 1840 many of the displaced tribes of eastern woodland Indians had been relocated in the Indian Territory, occupying what is now the eastern half of the state of Oklahoma. But the white man had not solved the Indian problem. He now faced a new kind of adversary—the Plains Indians.

Until the Spaniards introduced horses into North America, there had been no Plains Indians. As the number of horses increased, beginning in the 1700s, the abundant meat supplied by the vast herds of buffalo drew the Cheyenne and Sioux from the East, the Blackfoot from the North, the Pawnee and Comanche from the South and the Ute from the West into the Plains. The horses gave the Indians the mobility they needed to hunt buffalo and to cross the great stretches of arid land. Because of the horses, too, a new kind of Indian warfare developed, based, as always, on the Indians' expert scouting and hunting techniques, but with the added advantage of rapid movement and the ability to bring hundreds, and even thousands, of warriors together for a decisive battle.

Strangely enough, the Plains Indians did not begin serious warfare against the encroaching white settlers until almost twenty years after the first pioneers began the westward migration. True, they raided wagon trains and picked off individual hunters or small groups of trappers, but though a growing resentment against the invaders smoldered in the minds of the ambitious young braves, there was no full-scale resistance. When that resistance finally began, it was touched off by a senseless killing of friendly whites by four boisterous braves.

The Great Sioux Uprising began in Meeker County, Minnesota, on August 17, 1862. On that day, four young Dakota

Sioux rode through the small white settlement of Acton on their way back to their Rice Creek encampment after an unsuccessful hunting expedition. They were hungry and argumentative and began boasting of their bravery, taunting each other with being afraid of the white man. The taunting got more serious, and finally honor was at stake. Before they had finished proving to each other that they were not afraid of the white man, five settlers were dead. The Indians rode excitedly back to their encampment and leaped off their horses, shouting, "Get your guns! There's war with the whites and we have begun it!"

The Sioux were a nation of many tribes, and by dawn all the chiefs of the tribes in southwestern Minnesota had gathered for council at the house of a Medewakanton chief named Little Crow. As each chief spoke, the list of grievances against the whites grew longer, and the chiefs more insistent on war. Chief Red Middle Voice, seeing that Little Crow was not favorably inclined toward open warfare, used his most persuasive argument: He opened the door and let the assembled chiefs hear the howling of their war-thirsty braves. "They want to kill," said Red Middle Voice. "If the chiefs stand in the way, they will be the first to die." The arguments continued briefly, but the issue had been settled. With a brief nod of his head, Little Crow agreed to war. Without any chief actually saying the words, the general orders spread among the braves like wildfire. By the end of that day, more than four hundred white settlers in the area were dead.

Fort Ridgely was located on the Minnesota River at the southeast corner of the Lower Sioux Reservation. The fort was manned by Company C, Fifth United States Infantry, under the command of Captain John Marsh. When the first word of the Indian attacks reached Captain Marsh he passed them off as isolated raids rather than concerted attacks, but at the same time he knew he must reestablish order. Of a total of 125 men present for duty, 50 were off on patrol with Lieutenant Timothy Sheehan. Marsh took 46 men and set out for the Indian reservation by way of the Redwood Ferry. Twenty-nine men were left to defend the fort and the growing number of refugees who were gathering there for safety.

As they rode toward the ferry, the soldiers encountered several groups of panicky refugees and observed many mutilated bodies. Still Captain Marsh chose to believe that this had been the work of a single raiding party, working alone. Neither Marsh nor his elderly Indian interpreter noticed the occasional Indian scout silently watching them from the crest of a nearby hill or calmly riding parallel to their march. Once the column of soldiers had passed the last fork at which they could turn away from the ferry, the Indians knew their destination. One hundred braves took cover on each side of the ford, many of them swimming their horses across the "unfordable" river. When Captain Marsh and his men arrived at the crossing, they found the ferry boat on their side of the river, but the guiding ropes were loose. Some of the men dismounted to tighten them. Without warning, a signal shot was fired from the other side and the Indians unleashed their attack.

Only those soldiers who could reach the small thicket of brush near the river escaped the initial attack. Captain Marsh was one of them. By four o'clock in the afternoon of August 18, the survivors were trapped between Indians on three sides and the river on the fourth. Seeking an escape route, the captain and several soldiers tried to swim downstream. The captain was seized by a cramp and drowned. One by one the remaining swimmers were picked off. This diversion, however, permitted the rest of the survivors on shore to slip away and make their way back to the fort. By the small hours of the morning of August 19, twenty-three exhausted men had wandered into the post. An equal number of soldiers, plus the captain and the interpreter, had died.

During the attack at the ford, Little Crow's scouts had been moving in on Fort Ridgely to study the situation there. Since the fort was only a collection of buildings with no surrounding wall, the scouts were able to tether their horses out of sight and crawl into the fort itself. They lay patiently in the shadows counting every soldier, making sure they did not count the same ones twice. They counted the cannon, or "wagon guns," and noted their positions and the directions in which they were pointed. Finally they slipped back to their horses and rode quietly away to report to Little Crow.

While the scouts were doing their work, Little Crow had assembled three hundred warriors less than two miles from the fort, in plain sight of the watching defenders. After hearing the scouts' reports, he called all the chiefs to council and recommended an immediate attack on Fort Ridgely. He pointed out the large amount of food that was known to be stored in the fort's warehouse, the great supply of guns and powder locked in the stone powder magazine, and the growing herds of horses and cattle being driven in by the refugees.

But other chiefs wanted to bypass the fort and attack the town of New Ulm. The town was less than twenty miles away and, they argued, everything that Little Crow had said about the spoils in the fort was even more true about New Ulm. There were white men's stores with all kinds of unbelievable treasures there, and, most important, there were no soldiers at all. The arguing went on for hours.

Those hours of delay proved disastrous to the Sioux. Lieutenant Sheehan and his fifty-man patrol galloped back to the fort, and Sheehan took command as the senior surviving officer. Fifty Civil War volunteers from the town of St. Peter marched in on their way to Fort Snelling. Later in the day a group of hastily organized militia, also from St. Peter, swelled the defensive force at Fort Ridgely to more than 180 men. The arrival of the reinforcements at the fort was duly reported by the Indian scouts, and Little Crow was voted down. New Ulm would be the target for the next attack.

Two hundred warriors set out to attack New Ulm late that day, Tuesday, August 19. As they rode toward the town they found many settlers' cabins unburned and stopped to set them afire. They encountered a few white families who were not aware of the uprising and lingered to massacre them. A handful of braves reached New Ulm with little combative spirit left. After a brief skirmish with a sheriff's posse, the satiated warriors rode back to the encampment near Fort Ridgely.

Now the chiefs agreed to accept Little Crow's plan of attacking the fort. But the Indians had missed their chance. Even though they outnumbered the whites by three to one, the defenders of the fort were now well prepared, with plenty of canister shot to fire from the wagon guns. A half-hearted attack on Wednesday was repulsed easily. A heavier attack was made on Friday by more than eight hundred braves. It lasted six hours, but only one defender was killed.

Little Crow's intelligence had been good. If he had been able to act immediately on the reports from his scouts, Fort Ridgely would have been taken. But the need for a single commander was a hard lesson for proud tribal chiefs to accept.

This first large-scale outbreak of Indian warfare continued for some forty days. In that short time, at least eight hundred white settlers, militiamen, and soldiers were killed. The uprising collapsed, not because there had been any decisive victory by the whites, but because the Indians still lacked unity.

During the balance of the Civil War, Indian resentment against the whites continued to grow and spread over most of the frontier. The commanders of federal troops in the West, such as Colonel Kit Carson, had to divide their attention between Confederate raiders and marauding Indians. There is little doubt that harassment by the Indians drew federal troops away from the war and made life somewhat easier for the Confederates. There were very few significant actions against the Indians as long as the war continued. Large-scale operations against the Indians were finally undertaken in 1867 by an army of experienced regular soldiers. Ironically, it was the Sioux who once again touched off the hostilities by resisting the movement of settlers and supply trains up the Bozeman Trail, through their best hunting ground, to the Montana mining settlements.

With few exceptions, the officers of this new regular army had had enough experience and were sufficiently realistic to know that they needed the help of some real Indian-fighting experts. There were a few capable white frontiersmen around, like Bill Cody and Charlie Reynolds (General Custer's favorite white scout), but there were not enough of them to provide expert scouts and Indian-fighting advisors for all the army units. The next best choice seemed obvious. Who could fight Indians better than other Indians? In 1866, Secretary of War Stanton authorized the enlistment of Indian scouts.

There was no universal brotherhood among the Indians. For centuries the larger groups, like the Sioux, Cheyenne, and Comanche, had harassed the smaller ones, killing their hunters and kidnapping their women. Service with the white soldiers presented the lesser tribes with an opportunity for vengeance. Soon there were Crow, Pawnee, Arikara, Ree,

Early Apache scouts. Four are armed with the .58-caliber Springfield rifle that was the standard army weapon during the Civil War

and Shoshone scouts trailing the war parties of their hereditary enemies and leading the "Pony Soldiers" to their camps. Eventually, even the proud Apache scouted for the bluecoats. By the standards of the disciplined professional soldier, the performance of the Indian scouts was not always perfect, but they provided an invaluable service during the long years of Indian campaigning.

Three companies of Pawnee scouts were with the Fifth Cavalry in their campaign of 1869 during which Buffalo Bill Cody, the chief scout for the regiment, killed Chief Tall Bull. In the fateful summer of 1876, more than two hundred Crow and Shoshone scouts were with General Crook when he moved out against the Sioux and Cheyenne in his part of General Sheridan's master plan of entrapment. Colonel Wesley Merritt's Fifth Cavalry eventually became part of Crook's command and, of course, Bill Cody was with the Fifth.

It is fitting that the most famous battle of the Indian wars has become the best source of information about the ways in which the Indian scouts did their work. For years after the battle at the Little Big Horn, newspaper reporters, military historians, and relatives of soldiers killed with Custer sought out the survivors of the Seventh Cavalry, the friendly Indian scouts, and the victorious Sioux. For the first time, a significant amount of information was assembled from the testimony of the Indian participants of a battle. Some of the stories they told were over-simplified, as if the battle were not worth a detailed discussion. Some accounts rambled in many directions, but added interesting details. Some were calculated to make the storyteller a bigger, braver man than he really was. But by putting together the Indian accounts of all types, an unusual and interesting narrative develops—the Battle of the Little Big Horn, as described by the Indians.

On July 21, 1876, six Crow scouts joined the Seventh Cavalry, under the command of General Custer, at the juncture of the Yellowstone and Rosebud rivers. Custer told them he was going to fight the Sioux. "If we win the fight," said the general, "everything belonging to the enemy you can take home, for my boys have no use for these things."

What the Crows had no way of knowing was that Custer was defying his orders from General Terry. These orders stated that Custer was not to move into the area of the Little Big Horn until July 26, since the slower-moving elements of Terry's command could not reach there before that time. Custer's orders were to avoid an engagement with the Indians until the twenty-sixth, when reinforcements would be available if they were needed. The force of Sioux and Cheyenne he sought totaled almost four thousand of the finest Indian warriors, well armed, with plenty of ammunition and a good supply of horses. Custer had only six hundred men, and although he had been offered a battery of gatling guns to increase his firepower, he had grandly declined to bring them along, claiming that they would slow down his movement.

Scout White-Man-Runs-Him tells in his account how the Crows located the Sioux village and reported it to Custer, who then went with them to a lookout point.

As he watched the village Custer said, "These people are very troublesome and bother the Crows and white people. I am going to teach them a lesson today. I will whip them and will build a fort at the junction where the Little Horn flows into the Big Horn, and you Crows may then live in peace." He said he would finish the Sioux troubles.

The Indian scouts thought there were too many Sioux for Custer to fight, but since Sioux scouts had seen the soldiers there was no use trying to make a surprise attack. The scout showed Custer a path toward the Sioux camp that would keep the soldiers out of sight until they were ready to cross into the valley.

When they were about a mile from the mouth of Ash Creek, they saw dust rising near the mouth of the creek. Custer called the chief of the Crow scouts and asked what the dust was. The scout said, "The Sioux must be running away." Custer then ordered Major Reno to move to the south in case the Sioux tried to escape that way. White-Man-Runs-Him, with a half-breed Sioux named Mitch Boyer and three of the other Crow scouts, rode on ahead of Custer. His narrative continues:

We could see Custer and his brother move to the crest of a small hill to the right of us and wave their hats to the soldiers passing beneath them. The soldiers waved their hats and shouted. Because our ponies were smaller than the soldiers' horses we had to gallop to get ahead of the column again. We took a position on a bluff where we could look down into the Sioux camp.

Custer came down Medicine Tail Creek toward the river and the Sioux saw him there. They all began running that way. There were thousands of them. Custer tried to cross the river but could not. This was the last time we saw Custer. Mitch Boyer said to us, 'You scouts need go no further. You have guided Custer here, and your work is finished, so you had better go back to the pack train and let the soldiers do the fighting.' He said he was going down to join Custer and turning his horse, galloped away. This was the last time we saw Mitch Boyer.

We went back along the ridge and found Reno's men entrenched there. They had had a very hard fight. Many men were wounded. We stayed there all afternoon. It was hot and the soldiers had no water. When they got thirsty, some would volunteer to go down to the river to fill canteens. Many soldiers were killed trying to get water. After sundown I slipped through the Sioux lines and the next morning I was down where the Little Horn runs into the Big Horn. There were some soldiers there and their leader was a man whom the Indians call "Man Without Hip" [General Terry] and another officer whom the Indians call "White Whiskers" [Colonel Gibbon]. I told them all I knew about the fight. Then I told them that my clothes were worn out and I had no moccasins, so I was going home. The officers said all right and I rode on.

Of the total of about six hundred men present for duty with the Seventh Cavalry on June 25, 1876, Custer sent one-fourth galloping off with Reno and another group, almost as big, with Captain Benteen. To make matters worse, the entire supply of reserve ammunition was sent along behind Benteen with the pack train. Reno was engaged first and forced to retreat. Then Benteen and his command were attacked but were able to join Reno, who was entrenched on the ridge. They had plenty of ammunition and a good defensive position, but Custer had neither a good position nor any extra ammunition. His soldiers had only the bullets they carried in their cartridge belts and fifty rounds in their saddle bags. The entire command had gone into battle after an all-night march, so both horses and men were exhausted before the battle ever started.

The narrative is finished by Two Moon, a chief of the victorious Cheyenne. He picks it up as Custer forms his troops near the crest of a small ridge:

Then the Sioux rode up the ridge on all sides, riding very fast. The Cheyennes went up the left way. Then the shooting was quick, quick. Pop-pop-pop, very fast. Some of the soldiers were down on their knees, some standing. Officers all in front. The smoke was like a great cloud, and everywhere the Sioux went the dust rose like smoke. We circled all around them—swirling like water around a stone. We shoot, we ride fast, we shoot again. Soldiers drop and horses fall on them. Soldiers in line drop, but one man rides up and down the line—all the time shouting. He rode a sorrel horse with a white face and white forelegs. I don't know who he was. He was a brave man.

Indians keep swirling around and round, and the soldiers killed only a few. Many soldiers fell. At last all horses killed but five. Once in awhile some man would break out and run toward the river, but he would fall. At last about one hundred men and five horsemen stood on the hill all bunched together. All along the bugler kept blowing his commands. He was very brave too. Then a chief was killed. I hear it was Long Hair [Custer], I don't know; and then the five horsemen and the bunch of men, maybe some forty, started toward the river. The man on the sorrel horse led them, shouting all the time. He wore buckskin shirt and had long black hair and black mustache. He fought very hard with a big knife. His men were all covered with white dust. I couldn't tell whether they were officers or not. One man all alone ran far down toward the river, then round up over the hill. I thought he was going to escape, but a Sioux fired and hit him in the head. He was the last man. He wore braid on his arms.

The war with the Sioux continued for another fourteen years. Each year saw a dwindling number of military engagements as the strength of the Sioux nation was sapped by disease, hunger, and mismanagement on the part of the government Indian agents, who had no idea of what the Indians needed to stay healthy and to lead a normal life. A last token resistance was made at Wounded Knee, South Dakota, on December 28, 1890. A medicine man had aroused the warriors by chanting that their bullets would find white targets, but that the white man's bullets would be turned aside by the magic which had permeated their shirts during a Ghost Dance. A single warrior touched off this final slaughter by drawing his rifle from its hiding place under a blanket, raising it in consecration, and firing a shot in the direction of the soldiers. By an odd coincidence, the troops were from the Seventh Cavalry. The single shot was answered by volley after volley. When the shooting stopped, 145 Sioux warriors, women, and children were dead. The Seventh Cavalry lost 30 soldiers in this final action against their bitter enemies.

Although the Indian wars were actually at an end, the

army kept small detachments of Indian scouts with all its units that were stationed in what had once been Indian territory. The order that had permitted the enlistment of the first Indian scouts had specified that they would be paid the same as a private soldier, but made no mention of providing them with uniforms or permitting them to achieve any rank other than just "scout." Their status gradually improved, however. They were eventually given uniforms and were promoted within the enlisted ranks.

The Indian scouts had one last opportunity to fight as a distinct unit when General Pershing went campaigning in Mexico against the bandit-politician Francisco "Pancho" Villa. Following a series of minor border incidents, Villa's troops attacked the town of Columbus, New Mexico, on March 9, 1916. The Mexicans, known as "Villistas," suffered far heavier casualties than did the defending American troops, but the incident pushed the United States into the position of having to send troops into a neighboring sovereign nation to pursue a bandit.

The Mexican government under General Carranza officially agreed to the pursuit, but did little to help it. Carranzista troops, in fact, seemed to take delight in hindering the movement of the Americans. Pancho Villa, after all, was a sort of Mexican Robin Hood and Jesse James rolled into one. The Mexican people, even those whom he robbed, resented the presence of American troops, and resisted the Americans' attempts to gain intelligence from them. Chasing Villa became a sort of game. Pershing's units wore themselves out running after rumors. On any one day Villa might be reported in a dozen places, but while many of the reports resulted in skirmishes with Villista units, General Pancho was never caught.

Pershing's army was an odd mixture of the new and the old. His troops were mostly cavalry and infantry, looking very much like their predecessors of the Indian wars except for the olive drab color of their uniforms. They had the advantage, however, of the latest technological advances. Portable radio sets could send messages flashing over distances of three hundred miles—when their batteries were fully charged and the weather was right. Gasoline-powered trucks hauled men and supplies at unheard-of speeds—until they ran out of decent roads. The United States Army's entire fleet of aircraft was committed to the campaign. They proved to be a useful but fragile tool. Eight aircraft of the First Aero Squadron started the campaign, but only one was still flying when it was over.

The Apache scouts were perhaps the most anachronistic part of Pershing's Mexican Punitive Expedition. They seemed to be a throwback to another century, and yet they were more effective, in their own way, than the airplane or the motor truck. They were a little out of their element because this was essentially a white man's kind of war: There was a lot of chasing around before a battle and then there was a fight in which one side defended a fixed position while the attackers charged directly at them. This way of fighting was instinctively repugnant to the Apache. He believed that when you found an enemy you circled him, sniped at him every time he raised his head, and wore him down, without making any foolish headlong charges into his guns.

First Sergeant Chicken was in charge of the Apache scouts. He was just finishing his seventh enlistment and was a good, reliable soldier. Under him were two more fine noncommissioned officers, Sergeant Chow Big and his brother Corporal Monotolth. One of the ways in which the Apaches were most helpful was in getting information from reluctant Mexicans. There is no evidence that the Apaches used any form of physical torture, but they took maximum advantage of the Mexican's deep fear of them. The oldest of the scouts, Hell-Yet-Suey, practiced a kind of psychological warfare when he questioned prisoners.

Hell-Yet-Suey was a very old and very ugly hereditary Apache chief. His face was sunburned almost black. His eyes were always badly bloodshot and the lids drooped, giving him the appearance of a snake. His long black hair, usually coated with the dust of Mexico, hung down past his shoulders. He affected a sort of permanent grin, exposing yellowed teeth. When a reluctant Mexican was brought to him, the old Indian would say nothing, although he and the other Apaches all spoke Spanish. He would simply walk around the prisoner very slowly, getting ever closer until that awful face was pressed against the prisoner's. Depending on the way the prisoner reacted, this slow encirclement could take anywhere from a couple of minutes to several hours. Few Mexicans had courage enough to resist this silent torture when they knew that a few words would let them escape the awful specter confronting them.

The Indian scouts took part in their last fight on May 5, 1916, at the Ojos Azules ranch, three hundred miles inside Mexico. A force of Villistas had had a desultory fight with some unenthusiastic Carranzistas the day before, fifteen miles south of the town of San Antonio. Then they had retired to the Ojos Azules ranch for a rest. A squadron of the Eleventh Cavalry under Major Henry Howze set out to find the Villistas before they had a chance to escape into the mountains. Howze's advance guard was the Apache scout detachment under First Sergeant Chicken.

The scouts found the ranch without difficulty and reported to Howze that the Villistas were still there. Howze organized his command into three parts—one to attack the ranch frontally, and two others to circle the Mexicans to cut off their escape.

The noise of the approaching cavalry gave the Americans away, and the Villistas made a frantic attempt to escape, leaving about thirty riflemen atop the ranch house to slow down the enemy. The Apache scouts were with the troop that was making the frontal assault on the ranch, but as soon as they came under fire from the rooftop marksmen, Sergeant Chicken and his men instinctively dismounted to return the fire. They wanted no part of a mad charge into the face of blazing guns.

Although most of the Villistas escaped, forty-four were killed and many more wounded. No American soldiers, either white or Apache, were hurt. The Apache scouts had fought their last battle as a unit of the United States Army. First Sergeant Chicken gave his own appraisal of the engagement: "Huli! Damfine fight!"

8

Funston?
He Was Only a Scout

On May 1, 1898, while Commodore George Dewey, wearing a white golf cap, sipped tea on the bridge of his flagship, the Asiatic Squadron of the United States Navy attacked the Spanish Far Eastern Fleet in Manila Bay, Philippine Islands. Dewey's famous order, "You may fire when ready, Gridley," opened a brief two-hour battle which destroyed the Spanish squadron and thrust the United States into serious Far Eastern affairs for the first time. A war that had been undertaken by the United States to liberate neighboring Cuba had been extended seven thousand miles across the sea.

But Dewey's victory did not secure the Philippines for the United States. Some fifteen thousand Spanish soldiers still defended Manila. Naval squadrons from Great Britain, France, Germany, and Japan rode at anchor in the bay waiting to fill any void in the firm control of the islands. Emilio Aguinaldo, leader of the Filipino *insurrectos*, was ready to challenge any foreign nation which coveted his native islands.

On his own authority, Commodore Dewey permitted Aguinaldo to move into the Cavite Naval Base and take captured Spanish arms. This permission was interpreted by the Filipino leader as a sign that the United States would grant the islands their independence, once the Spaniards had been driven out. This was not the case, of course, and no such pledge was ever made. The *insurrectos* joined the American troops sent to complete the defeat of the Spanish forces.

The first contingent of United States troops arrived at Cavite on July 1. They were poorly organized, ill-equipped, and led by men who had little appreciation of the political situation in the islands. Their commanding general did nothing to help the situation. Major General Wesley Merritt, former colonel of the Fifth United States Cavalry, was then sixty-two years old and far more enamored with the idea of retirement than with the prospect of another campaign to be fought in this far-away corner of the world. Merritt visited Cavite only once during his period of command, and there is no evidence that he ever met Emilio Aguinaldo.

The city of Manila was surrendered to the Americans on August 13, 1898, following a "sham" battle which was staged to preserve the honor of the Spanish governor. Relations between the Filipinos and their American "liberators" went slowly from bad to bitterly hostile. The United States Senate could not get enough votes to ratify the peace treaty with Spain, and the Filipinos interpreted this delay as a sign that the Americans had no intention of establishing a peaceful administration of the islands. Emilio Aguinaldo grew in power and prestige, issuing proclamations as president of a provisional republic and forming an army for the inevitable clash with the Americans.

Aguinaldo's army had few weapons, no trained leaders, and little organization. Its strength lay in the Filipinos' desire for freedom and in their knowledge of their islands. The semiorganized mobs that passed for "regular" troops were backed by a home guard of women and old men armed with spears, bows and arrows, and an occasional shotgun.

The *Sandatahan*, a small body of daredevil patriots, was organized as a sort of guerrilla unit to attack the Americans within Manila. These men were armed only with long bolo knives, daggers, or any sharp instrument they could find.

By the end of January 1899, forty thousand native residents of Manila had fled the city. Aguinaldo's army of thirty thousand men in the outskirts had fewer than ten thousand firearms. American patrols were being ambushed and cut to pieces with bolos. On February 4 an exchange of shots between American guards and a group of taunting Filipino soldiers precipitated a general outbreak of gunfire all around the periphery of the city. The next morning, February 5, the Americans began offensive operations.

Among the American units that went into action on February 5 was the Twentieth Kansas Volunteer Infantry Regiment. Its commander was Colonel Frederick Funston. A small, wiry man with seemingly boundless energy, Funston was highly respected by his men and by the senior officers. He had studied botany at the University of Kansas, made scientific expeditions to Death Valley and Alaska, and then, moved by the plight of the oppressed Cubans, had volunteered to join them in their revolt against Spain. After two years of hard campaigning, he was a lieutenant colonel and a sick man. He had returned to Kansas to recuperate.

When the United States entered the war against Spain, the governor of Kansas chose Funston to command one of the volunteer regiments to be raised in that state. Funston reminded the governor that he had had no formal military training, but the governor persisted and the colonel of the Twentieth Kansas Volunteers left for Topeka to join his regiment.

The war with Spain ended before the Twentieth saw any action, but just as they were about to be mustered out, they were ordered to the Philippines to assist in the "occupation."

Funston and his men arrived in Manila late in November 1898, and joined the command of General Arthur MacArthur. On the afternoon of February 5, 1899, the regiment helped add to the consternation of the Filipinos by making a head-on bayonet charge into a well-fortified position, driving out the defenders and then pursuing them for two miles into the jungle.

If there had ever been any serious doubt that the United States would take possession of the Philippines, this outbreak of fighting removed it. Even newspapers that had favored Philippine independence changed their position. The *New York Times* editorialized:

> The Filipinos have chosen a bloody way to demonstrate their incapacity for self-government . . . the insane attack of these people upon their liberators . . . To commit to their unsteady hands and childish minds political powers . . . would be to give a dynamite cartridge to a baby for a play-thing.

The Filipinos were once again *insurrectos,* fighting a guerrilla war against the self-constituted authority of the Americans. Emilio Aguinaldo was their leader, and his capture became the objective of the American offensive. Late in April, Colonel Funston's troops fought their way into the city of Malolos, which had been Aguinaldo's provisional capital, only to find the Hall of Congress and the presidential residence in flames. Aguinaldo and his government had escaped.

On April 27, the Twentieth Kansas reached the banks of the Rio Grande near Calumpit to find enemy guerrilla forces entrenched on the opposite side. Pulling a stout rope behind them, two American soldiers swam the river under the covering fire of the best marksmen in the regiment. The rope was made fast to a bamboo support of the Filipino's breastworks. Funston and seven men then climbed aboard a raft and pulled themselves across the river along the rope. While two men took the raft back for the next load, Funston and the remaining five soldiers leaped into the Filipino trench and captured all the guerrillas who had not fled under the unexpected attack of the crazy Americans. Funston and his two swimmers were awarded the Medal of Honor for their actions, and while marching back toward Manila, Funston learned that he had been promoted to brigadier general of volunteers.

The six-month tour of the volunteer regiments expired in May 1899, and they were replaced by regular troops. Funston returned to the United States with his regiment, sadly expecting to be mustered out with them. To his surprise and pleasure, he found that the War Department had decided to keep him on active service. He returned to Manila in December.

In the intervening months the nature of the war had changed. There was little large-scale action on either side. The Filipinos had learned that they could not match the Americans in formal battles, so they had split up their forces into small groups and were conducting guerrilla-type operations. The Americans, in turn, had learned that little was accomplished by marching out from Manila, capturing a town, then marching back to the city. As soon as the troops marched out of the town, the guerrillas filtered back in and took control again. The American scheme to meet this type of warfare was to divide the country into geographical areas, each with its own commander and troops. Each commander was responsible for ferreting out the guerrillas in his district and for gradually bringing the whole area under his control. General Funston was again assigned to General MacArthur's division and given command of the Third Brigade. In keeping with the new system of campaigning, the Third Brigade headquarters was at San Isidro in Nueva Ecija Province, while the fighting elements were scattered throughout that province as well as parts of Pangasinan and Pampanga provinces.

One of the very first things the new commander of the Third Brigade did after his arrival at San Isidro was to form a group of hand-picked soldiers into a unit known as the "Headquarters Scouts." These men were all picked for their horsemanship, ability with a rifle, and knowledge of scouting techniques. Many of them had been cowpunchers before joining the army. All were adventuresome, and all were fiercely loyal to Frederick Funston.

As one might expect from his background and previous behavior, Brigadier General Funston had no intention of directing the campaign from San Isidro. He was almost constantly in the field with his scouts, running down bits of intelligence that indicated the hiding place of a group of guerrillas or a cache of guerrilla supplies. At first, the local residents were suspicious of the energetic little general and were reluctant to give him information. Gradually, as he proved himself to be trustworthy, the flow of information improved.

Funston knew that simply killing a lot of Filipinos who were farmers by day and guerrillas by night would accomplish little. His real targets were the leaders of the guerrilla bands and the weapons with which they fought. Every officer sent to Manila as a prisoner or killed on the battlefield meant the loss of an irreplaceable commodity for the guerrillas—leadership. Every rifle or pistol and every single cartridge that fell into American hands shortened the insurrection. Funston reported his operations in terms of leaders eliminated or weapons captured. He found no pleasure in running up a big score of dead Filipinos.

This was the pattern of the war for more than a year. The opponents struck at each other whenever the opportunity presented itself. The Americans followed every lead into the jungles, swamps, and mountains in search of guerrilla bands. The guerrillas ambushed the searching Americans, raided their supply bases, and intimidated Filipino officials who took the oath of allegiance to the United States. They sought to maintain the level of fear by assassinating these officials or their families. The Americans sought to establish control by dealing swiftly with any captured guerrilla who had taken a part in the program of intimidation. The more brutal of the guerrillas were well known to the Americans, and Funston reported that, once they were captured, punishment was meted out quickly—at the end of a picket rope thrown over a convenient tree limb. Funston felt no particular compunction about this swift justice, but experienced agonizing remorse whenever a battle between American soldiers and a guerrilla band resulted in casualties among Filipino women and children.

No end was in sight as General Funston sat in his headquarters in San Isidro on the morning of February 8, 1901. Then a telegram arrived from an outlying garrison announcing that a band of guerrillas had surrendered, and that the leader of the band was carrying what appeared to be dispatches from the phantomlike Emilio Aguinaldo to his subordinate commanders. Funston knew that the whereabouts of the guerrilla leader had been the most earnestly sought-after piece of intelligence. He ordered the prisoners and the dispatches brought to him as quickly as possible, and when they arrived two days later, the general himself questioned their leader, Cecilio Segismundo. The guerrilla officer glibly told Funston that Aguinaldo was in hiding in the town of Palanan, a few miles inland from the east coast of northern Luzon. The revelation was made so freely that Funston became suspicious and decided that he would have to decipher the dispatches in an attempt to confirm Segismundo's information.

Assisted by an aide and by Lazaro Segovia, a Spaniard who had served the Americans as an intelligence operative for more than a year, Funston attempted to break the code. They labored for twenty consecutive hours before they discovered the key word to the cipher. The code was basically in Tagalog, the predominant Filipino dialect, but before it could be accurately translated into English it was first necessary to translate it into Spanish. With the code broken, the weary men stayed at work until all the captured documents were deciphered and translated. They contained much valuable material and ample evidence that they were in fact from Aguinaldo, but nowhere was there the slightest mention of Aguinaldo's hiding place. Funston was forced to accept Segismundo's information, but he felt more confident when the prisoner agreed to come over to the Americans and assist in a project to capture his former leader.

Funston and his weary assistants finally went to bed, but the general could not sleep. The germ of an idea had formed in his mind. One of the translated documents had been a request from Aguinaldo for a company of troops to be sent to him by various subordinate commanders, including Urbano Lacuna, the guerrilla leader in Funston's own area. Funston wondered if he could not arrange to send a group of his own men to Aguinaldo disguised as the requested reinforcements. But whom could he find to disguise as guerrillas? Certainly no group of American soldiers could pass as Filipinos. He decided to rely on the Macabebes, a group of Mexican Indian fighters brought into the Philippines by the Spanish many years earlier, who had now transfered their loyalty to the United States. They would be accompanied by some American officers disguised as prisoners.

By morning the basic plan was pretty well thought out. Funston had learned from the initial questioning of Segismundo that natives who lived in the area of Palanan watched the roads carefully for strangers and reported all movements to Aguinaldo. Funston had already decided that he would approach Palanan from the sea rather than be exposed to the scrutiny of the natives during a long overland march.

A written outline of the plan was sent to General MacArthur in Manila. When the division commander had examined the outline he sent for Funston and asked him to give a more detailed explanation.

According to Funston's plan, the main body of the expedition would be a company of Macabebe scouts. There was little love lost between the Macabebes and the native, Tagalog-speaking Filipinos, but to make the group seem natural, only Macabebes who could speak passable Tagalog would be taken along. Three native Filipinos, loyal to the United States, would act as their officers. Their American uniforms and rifles were to be taken away from them, and they would be clothed and armed like any group of *insurrectos*. Segovia and Segismundo would mingle with the company without any particular disguise, and marching along with the column, supposedly under heavy guard, would be five prisoners uniformed as privates in the United States Army. These would be General Funston, his aide, an infantry captain who had campaigned in the Palanan area, and the two American officers who were regularly assigned to the Macabebe Scout Company.

Once ashore in the vicinity of Palanan, Funston would send Aguinaldo two forged letters, supposedly from Urbano Lacuna, telling the guerrilla leader that some of his reinforcements were close by. The forgeries would be hard to discern since Funston had captured a quantity of Lacuna's stationery, and he had employed a skilled forger to copy Lacuna's signature. It was hoped that these letters would cause the natives along the coast to assist the supposed guerrillas and would identify the expedition to the complex of information gatherers serving Aguinaldo.

General MacArthur approved the plan and made arrangements with the navy to provide the gunboat *Vicksburg* for the trip to the northern end of Luzon. At this point only Funston, Segovia, and General MacArthur knew the purpose of the trip or the final destination. Segismundo was not informed until the *Vicksburg* had sailed.

It took three weeks to make the final preparations. Each of the Macabebes was tested to make sure of his ability to speak Tagalog, and Funston carefully eliminated any of them who might not be able to stand the physical rigors he expected. Eighty-one of the one hundred little "Macs" in the company were selected to go along. The insurgent clothing and a typical assortment of weapons were put aboard the *Vicksburg* under the cover of darkness. Finally, with everything ready, Funston called on General MacArthur to pay his respects before embarking. The division commander's parting words were not very encouraging. "Funston," he said, "this is a desperate undertaking. I fear that I shall never see you again."

On the night of March 6, 1901, the *Vicksburg*, with its strange group of passengers, slipped out of Manila Bay and headed northward. Once safely away from land, Funston told the captain of the ship and his own American officers their ultimate destination and the purpose of their expedition. Next, he and Segovia called for the three Filipino officers, all former *insurrectos*, reminded them that they had taken the oath of allegiance to the United States, and then informed them that they were going after their former leader. The Filipinos were shocked by this unexpected announcement, but they eventually recovered their composure and comported themselves well throughout the entire expedition. The senior of the three Filipinos was Hilario Tal Placido, who had been captured in a battle with Funston's own Twentieth Kansas regiment. He now bore the uncertain honor of nominally commanding a force which sought to capture a hero of his own nation.

When the "little Macs" were told their mission they were immediately enthusiastic, but some of this enthusiasm melted away when they were told to turn in their fine American uniforms and Krag carbines in exchange for the odd assortment of rags and weapons that were part of their disguise. Their good humor soon returned, however, as they were told additional details of the mission. A description of the way the American officers were to be herded like prisoners whenever they were near a town brought howls of anticipatory laughter.

As the *Vicksburg* approached its destination, Funston and Segovia busied themselves with preparing the text of the bogus letters to Aguinaldo. They produced two masterpieces of deception which would calm any fears the *insurrecto* leader might have about a force of armed men coming toward his hideaway. The letters would be sent to Aguinaldo once the expedition was ashore.

On the night of March 14, the *Vicksburg* steamed toward the coast with all its lights screened from view. The general had decided to land at night, so that the gunboat could be away and out of sight by dawn. At about one o'clock on the morning of the fifteenth, the ship entered Casiguran Bay and the crew began putting its boats over the side. The darkness was compounded by a heavy rain that provided better cover than expected, but also got the expedition off to a damp and chilly start.

It was a sad-looking group that stood on the rain-soaked

beach. The Macabebes and their officers looked forlorn in their cast-off rags. The Americans were described by Funston as "a pretty scrubby-looking bunch of privates. There is a lot in clothes, after all." While it was still dark, they moved up the coast to a point at which a force that had actually come overland might have stopped. There they found fresh water and built fires to cook their ration of rice. Like typical guerrillas, they carried only enough food to last one day.

As the little force made its way along the coast toward the town of Casiguran, they had to follow the indentations of the very irregular shoreline. Most of the time the tide was high and they were forced to wade through many inlets. In one of these inlets they discovered a small *banca* (a native boat) and devised a plan to make good use of it. Funston and Segovia concocted another one of their letters, this time addressed to the *presidente,* or mayor, of Casiguran. It informed the *presidente* that a force of insurgent troops, on its way to report to Aguinaldo, was just south of Casiguran and its commander desired a guide to lead them into town. It also asked that preparations be made to feed and house the insurgents in Casiguran. Hilario Tal Placido signed the letter, since he was to be playing the role of commander. Segismundo, with one of the Filipino officers and two Macabebes set out for Casiguran in the *banca*.

The guide met them at about four o'clock in the afternoon, thus giving them the assurance that their letter to the *presidente* had been delivered and accepted as genuine. They entered the town to the accompaniment of the town band and were treated to a hero's welcome. A few ominous glances were cast in the direction of the American "prisoners" but they were not mistreated. The *presidente* had ordered several buildings cleared as quarters for the patriotic troops, but he had bad news about procuring food for the balance of the hundred-mile journey to Palanan. Little rice was produced in this area, he informed Tal Placido. The people preferred a diet of cracked corn, fish, and sweet potatoes. There was hardly any corn available at the moment, the sweet potatoes were too bulky to carry on a long overland march, and the fish, obviously, would spoil quickly in the heat. The *presidente* hoped that if the patriots could wait four or five days, he might be able to find enough cracked corn to supply them. But Funston had arranged to rendezvous with the *Vicksburg* at Palanan Bay on March 25 and he could not wait. He decided to push on and trust to the good luck they had had up to now. Tal Placido informed the *presidente* that they would leave the next day, and the well-intentioned official bullied the town into giving up four hundred pounds of cracked corn—enough to last about four days.

Funston and Segovia composed still another letter, this one a sort of progress report to Aguinaldo, and the helpful *presidente* provided runners to carry it to Palanan, together with the two written on board the *Vicksburg*. On the morning of March 17, the Macabebes and their "prisoners" started on the longest and hardest leg of their journey. The helpful *presidente* provided a guide and twelve townsmen to act as porters and even accompanied them himself for the first couple of miles.

There was no road or trail up the coast toward Palanan. The little expedition made its way along the beach, whenever there was one, and through the rock-strewn jungle the rest of the time. The presence of the porters from Casiguran made it necessary to constantly maintain the fiction of the American prisoners for fear that a slip would cause the Casigurans to send a warning to Aguinaldo.

Rain fell steadily for five days. Their supply of cracked corn soon became a smelly, fermented mess, but it was all they had. The Macabebes were sometimes able to catch small fish with their bare hands and they were always on the lookout for snails and limpets. Whenever they stopped long enough to coax a fire out of the damp wood, everything— fish, snails, limpets, and sour corn—would go into the pot together. Sleep was almost impossible since the men had nothing to lie on or to keep off the rain. It was no wonder that by the end of the fifth day the men were faint from hunger and exhaustion, so that the column of a hundred straggled out for over a mile.

At five in the afternoon of the fifth day, they saw a man standing on the beach ahead of them, obviously watching their progress. Segovia limped out ahead of the column, favoring a badly ulcerated foot, and greeted the man, who handed him a letter. Segovia limped back to the column and, as he passed Funston, whispered in Spanish, "It is all right. We have them." As it turned out, they were only ten miles from Palanan and their deception had not been detected.

The letter given to Segovia was written by Simon Villa, Aguinaldo's chief of staff, to "Lieutenant Colonel Hilario Tal Placido," and showed that the insurgents had been entirely taken in by the letters sent from Casiguran. The only disturbing part of the letter from Villa was an order to Tal Placido to leave the Americans under guard in a place called Dinundungan, which was just two miles up the beach. Funston's sense of humor had returned a little. He commented, "Just think of living in a place with such a name as that!"

When they straggled into Dinundungan, they found a little old native man busily engaged in building a hut to hold the prisoners. They were now just eight miles from their goal. Eight miles of comparatively easy walking down a well-marked path and they would be at Aguinaldo's hide-away. But how were they to finish the job with the Americans shut up in their prison hut and ten men left behind to "guard" them? Another forged letter solved the problem.

The expedition rested at Dinundungan overnight. Then dawn came of the day they had been waiting for. With Segovia and Tal Placido in the lead, the main column started down the trail toward Palanan. Two hours later a couple of Macabebes came back down the trail to Dinundungan with the bogus letter that countermanded the original order to leave the Americans behind. The old man could read and he was satisfied that the new order was genuine, but he complained that they needn't have put him to the trouble of building the hut if they hadn't intended to use it. The five Americans and their ten-man "guard" set out for Palanan at once.

Although they had breakfasted on good cracked corn that morning, Funston and one of the other Americans were still quite weak and had to rest every few hundred yards. They were about halfway to Palanan when a Macabebe sergeant came running back down the trail toward them, motioning them off the trail. No sooner were they hidden than a group of real guerrillas came around a bend, headed toward Dinundungan. After they were safely past the Americans' hiding place, the Macabebe sergeant explained that the guerrillas had been sent back to relieve the ten men guarding the prisoners so that all of the "reinforcements" could come to Palanan. The quick-witted Segovia, upon encountering this group on the trail, had managed to delay them long enough for the Macabebe sergeant to reach Funston with the warning.

At this point, the success of the entire expedition depended on the way Segovia and Tal Placido conducted themselves. Funston and the other Americans could not permit themselves to be seen. They deliberately stayed some distance behind the main column. Fortunately, the guerrillas who had been sent to Dinundungan did not return to give the alarm.

About a mile from Palanan a guerrilla officer came out to meet the column. He escorted them to a ferry crossing on the Palanan River and then invited Segovia and Tal Placido to accompany him to Aguinaldo. Placido ordered his men to follow him into town as fast as the ferry could bring them over. A few minutes later, he and Segovia were shaking hands with Emilio Aguinaldo and being congratulated on their determined march from Nueva Ecija. The two exhausted men found themselves in the company of seven of Aguinaldo's most stalwart supporters, each well armed. The house was surrounded by a guard of fifty neatly uniformed guerrillas armed with Mauser rifles.

Hilario Tal Placido regaled Aguinaldo and his followers with wild tales about their experiences during the journey while Segovia stared out the window, seemingly bemused but actually watching for the arrival of the Macabebes. After a wait that seemed much too long, the Macabebes marched up under the command of their other officers and formed ranks facing Aguinaldo's troops. Just as Tal Placido seemed to be running out of amusing stories, Segovia leaned out the window and signaled to the Macabebes. "Now is the time, Macabebes!" shouted one of their officers. "Give it to them!"

The poor "little Macs" were exhausted and nervous. The best they could manage was a ragged volley in the general direction of Aguinaldo's guard, which killed two of the guards and wounded Aguinaldo's bandmaster, who just happened to be walking by. But the result of this unexpected development was utter panic among the guards. They ran in every direction.

Aguinaldo interpreted the volley as some kind of a welcoming salute and he stepped to the window shouting, "Stop that foolishness! Don't waste your ammunition!" Then

Some of Funston's Macabebe scouts, after their mission
to capture Aquinaldo

as he realized what had happened and sprang back from the
window, Tal Placido grabbed him, threw him under a table,
and sat on him. Segovia opened fire on several of Aguinaldo's
officers, who tried to draw their pistols. The shots wounded
Simon Villa and one other officer. The remaining officers
leaped out of the window and escaped. With Aguinaldo
securely pinned under the table, Tal Placido proudly an-
nounced, "You are the prisoner of the Americans."

Funston and his little party had reached the river just as the shots were fired by the Macabebes. They frantically commandeered a *banca* and paddled rapidly across the stream. They were met on the opposite bank by an excited Segovia, splattered with the blood of the men he had wounded. He called out in Spanish, "It is all right. We have him!" Funston ran to the house as fast as he could and introduced himself to Aguinaldo. He then explained the identity of the "reinforcements" and made sure that Aguinaldo realized he was a prisoner of war. Funston described Aguinaldo at that moment: "He said in a dazed sort of way, 'Is this not some joke?' I assured him that it was not, though, as a matter of fact, it was a pretty bad one on him. While naturally agitated, his bearing was dignified, and in this moment of his fall there was nothing of the craven. He is a man of many excellent qualities, far and away the best Filipino I ever was brought in contact with."

Early on the morning of March 25, 1901, the captors of Aguinaldo, with their very valuable prize, set out for the Bay of Palanan. It was not easy going, since many of the Macabebes had badly bruised and cut feet, but they arrived at the bay about noon to see the smoke of the approaching gunboat rising over the horizon. When the *Vicksburg* was standing about two miles off shore Funston used a torn bedsheet to wigwag, "We have him. Send boats for all." From the ship came the response, "Well done."

To Funston came a letter from the vice-president of the United States:

Oyster Bay, March 30, 1901

My Dear General:

This is no perfunctory or formal letter of congratulation. I take pride in this crowning exploit of a career filled with feats of cool courage, iron endurance and gallant daring

... I cannot recall any single feat in our history which can be compared to it ...

Faithfully yours,
Theodore Roosevelt

By the middle of May all organized insurgent activity had ceased. The movement for Philippine independence had lost its leader and rallying point, Emilio Aguinaldo. By November Funston was gone, too. The Kansas volunteer was sent home as a brigadier general in the regular army and was later promoted to major general. He served with distinction until his untimely death in 1917 at the age of fifty-two. The old-line regular officers never fully accepted him, though. When asked about the captor of Aguinaldo they would reply, "Funston? He was only a scout."

9

Scouting
"No Man's Land"

Nothing in the American frontier tradition could have prepared men for the type of warfare they experienced in France during 1917 and 1918.

The Great War had begun in 1914 as a classic piece of mobile warfare. The French moved an army of 200,000 men into an area just west of the Belgian and Luxembourg borders, knowing that the Germans would surely attack but uncertain about the path the attack would follow. The Germans ended the uncertainty on August 4 by launching an all-out offensive into Belgium. The brave little Belgian army delayed the Germans long enough for the British to mobilize their regular army and move it to France, but by August 23 the great Belgian fortress at Liège had fallen, Brussels had been captured, and the armies of Imperial Germany were marching into France.

The French military philosophy of that time was one of counterattack: let the enemy penetrate your defenses a little, get him off balance and perhaps a little overconfident, and then strike back swiftly and hard! On September 5 the French armies under Marshal Joffre struck back. With typical French *élan*, or spirit, the men under "Papa" Joffre hurled themselves against the Germans. The famous French cuirassiers, mounted on the best horses and wearing their gleaming ceremonial breastplates and plumed helmets, drove into the German flanks, stinging the field gray monster with their sabers. The juggernaut was gradually slowed, halted at the Marne River, and then sent into retreat. Eventually the battle lines were stabilized along the Aisne River northeast of Paris. By the end of 1914, both sides had struck their greatest blows and the war settled down along a 450-mile "front" from the English Channel to Switzerland. In the next three years that front never varied by more than twenty miles at any given point, but more than a million men died.

The war became one of attrition: a contest to see which side could inflict the greatest number of casualties and the largest amount of damage on the other side. Both the Allied French and British armies and the Germans assembled thousands of cannon, large and small, which could reach out to strike any lucrative target. The role of the airplane, and even of the zeppelin, grew increasingly important. At Ypres, in April 1915, the Germans introduced poison gas to warfare and the Allies responded in kind. Tanks made their first appearance on the battlefield when the Allies introduced them in July 1915, but they were used as moving pillboxes, not to add an element of tactical mobility.

Gradually the area between the opposing armies became a wasteland. Towns, forests, and anything that stood above ground level were worn down by constant bombardment. The soldiers on both sides became moles, digging into the ground for protection. Contending lines of trenches faced each other, sometimes as close as fifty and rarely more than five hundred yards apart. Under the cover of darkness, the defenders of each trench line would move forward a little and erect barbed-wire entanglements to slow down any possible enemy attack. This work was made hazardous by the sweeping random fire of machine guns and by the sharp eyes of snipers, who watched for any movement revealed by the light of flares from the artillery. In the daytime the ill-considered act of raising a helmet above the trench parapet could bring anything from a single sniper's bullet to an artillery barrage. This barren, shell-pocked strip of land between the armies was known as No Man's Land. No American scout had ever faced anything like it.

In 1917 the Americans arrived in France full of spirit but ill-equipped to fight under the conditions they found. The army was desperately short of machine guns and had no airplanes of any operational value. A reasonably good supply of artillery pieces was available, but they were of odd calibers and would not fire either French or British ammunition. There was no stockpile of artillery ammunition in the United States and no industrial capability to turn it out fast enough. Machine guns came from the British; the French contributed aircraft, artillery, and ammunition. Special schools were set up to teach the Americans how to use the foreign equipment. Today, more than fifty years later, the United States Army still uses artillery pieces that are modern versions of those provided by the French.

Gradually the Americans were moved from their training areas in the rear to positions alongside experienced Allied units in quiet sectors of the front.

The First Infantry Division was the first major United States Army unit sent to the front. The division moved into the quiet Luneville sector in October 1917, and began training under realistic conditions. They soon found that even a "quiet" sector had its moments of terror when unexpected volleys of German artillery shells rained down in the midst of a period of calm. They were exposed to the grim, very unglamorous side of war when those sudden bombardments caught a group of men or a train of horse-drawn wagons moving along a road.

Allied teachers continued to school the Americans for real action against the Germans. They were taught that in an assault on an enemy trench, a hand grenade is much more effective than a rifle. They learned to creep and crawl under barbed-wire entanglements and to blend into every slight fold in the earth as they crawled. They drilled for hours to master the tricky business of getting their gas masks on in ten seconds. "Once you hear the gas alarm, stop breathing, mate, and get yer ruddy mask on! If yer tykes a breath, yer bloody well a goner!" Their English sergeant instructor knew—he had been gassed at Ypres.

When the time came to be schooled in the techniques of patrolling No Man's Land, the Americans found that even a small patrol was not a simple proposition. There was much planning to be done; a lot of coordination with nearby units was necessary to make sure that friendly patrols were not fired upon. Often there was a full-scale rehearsal when the patrol was of special importance.

A series of trenches would be dug somewhere to the rear of the front which exactly copied the friendly and enemy trenches in the area to be scouted. Identical barbed-wire obstacles were set up. The patrol might be rehearsed for several nights, until every man was able to find his way around that make-believe battleground in the dark, locate the right enemy trench, and get back to friendly trenches.

Since almost all patrols were conducted at night, when sounds travel much farther, silence was the watchword. Steel helmets were left behind, along with any small piece of equipment that might rattle. The scouts were taught to fight silently with their bayonets, their hands, or with a lethal little weapon known as a trench knife. This was a short-bladed stabbing knife with a handle in the form of a massive pair of brass knuckles. In a close fight its user could kill with a blow to the head from his brass-clad knuckles, or rip his adversary open with the blade.

But the Americans still had not heard of a new variation on a patrol, the raid. This operation was usually a little bigger than a patrol, and it had a harassing mission as well as one of gathering information. Whereas a patrol sought to avoid becoming involved in a fight, the raiders went out looking for one. They preferred to bring their intelligence home in the form of prisoners, which meant that they had to go right into the enemy trenches or waylay an enemy patrol to make a capture.

The larger raids were conducted with an artillery bombardment to prepare the way, as in a regular attack. Experienced troops in the front line trenches could tell when a raid was coming at them by the local nature of the shelling. The accepted technique for defense, once a raid was diagnosed, was to move back from the forward trenches. Then, while the raiders were searching the abandoned trenches for prisoners, the defenders would bring artillery fire in on them. When the raiders finally withdrew, the defenders simply moved back to their old positions. Of course, there were some instances in which a supposed raid was really an attack intended to hold the captured trench. This embarrassing situation forced the defenders to write the trench off as a loss, or to make an immediate counterattack to regain possession of it.

The winter of 1917–18 was a miserable one for the Americans. There were no major battles, but they were very much involved in the constant danger, monotony, and discomfort of trench warfare. Each side conducted just enough offensive operations to keep the other on the alert and to force him to keep his trenches fully manned and defended.

Finally winter ended and spring came. Then the pace of operations began to pick up. March found the Twenty-sixth Infantry Regiment of the First Infantry Division in the trenches near the town of Rambucourt in the Toul sector.

Two American scouts examine a German observation post in France in 1917. The post had recently been abandoned by the enemy

The regimental intelligence officer suspected that a German listening post, somewhere in the middle of No Man's Land, was hearing and seeing too much. The regimental commander decided to send a patrol to find the listening post. His decision may have been influenced by the fact that the regiment had not yet captured any German prisoners. In any case, the leader of the patrol, Lieutenant Christopher Holmes, was instructed to find the post and knock it out, and to bring in a prisoner in the process.

Lieutenant Holmes and Sergeant John Murphy set out with three other men. An early full moon had risen as they crawled over the top of their trench and headed out into the shambles of the battlefield. The intelligence officer had given them a general idea of the area in which the outpost was located, but once they had gone out past recognizable landmarks, Lieutenant Holmes found he had to use a compass to maintain the proper direction. The bright moon was helpful to them in avoiding old wire and other obstacles, but they knew that the same moonlight aided the enemy snipers who might be looking for the slightest movement. They crawled for about two hundred yards and then decided that they were screened from enemy view by a low ridge. They got to their feet and walked in a crouch. Suddenly the night was brightened by the white light of a star flare.

The Americans threw themselves flat on the ground, motionless. Sergeant Murphy felt himself begin to slide down into a shell crater, but he did not dare to check the slide for fear his thrashing might be seen. He came to rest gently at the bottom of the crater just as another flare lit the sky. His eyes had been closed in fear, but he opened them to look around. The empty eyes of a human skull, half hidden under a rusty German helmet, stared at him from a distance of a few inches. He leaped to his feet in terror and clawed his way up the side of the crater.

Lieutenant Holmes held his men in place for a few minutes until they could be sure that no more flares were going to be fired, and to let Sergeant Murphy collect his wits. Then they moved on toward their objective. Fifty yards farther on they ran into a fresh barbed-wire entanglement which indicated that they were near an occupied position. One of the scouts moved forward with a pair of wire cutters and clipped all twelve strands of wire, making sure that he held the loose ends so they could not spring back and make a noise. The patrol moved through the gap in the wire in single file. Holmes stopped to check his compass and to figure out where they were. The moonlight brightened as a cloud drifted off its path, and they saw, no more than ten feet away, the outpost! A German soldier stood looking almost directly at the patrol but apparently he had not seen them.

Without pausing to think, Holmes threw himself forward at the German and wrestled him down into the muddy water at the bottom of the dugout. The man soon ceased struggling when the point of a trench knife was placed against his throat. He begin to murmur, "Kamerad! Kamerad!"

Holmes quickly gathered the patrol and started back toward friendly lines. For some reason, the prisoner seemed to get more frightened as they worked their way back through the wire and shell craters and as they approached the American trenches, he began to shout, "Kamerad! Kamerad!" The cries drew random rifle fire from his own lines, but no one was hit. Lieutenant Holmes and his patrol gave the password as they approached a friendly outpost, and finally slid into their own trenches, dragging their prisoner along behind them.

The use of the password was a very important part of scouting No Man's Land. While a patrol was at work in the darkness, the individual members could use it to identify someone who came crawling toward them. When the work had been completed, the password was used for identification as the patrol approached friendly lines. A sentry, hearing someone moving toward him, would call, "Halt! Who's there?" and the patrol leader or individual scout would respond with the password for the day.

With the coming of spring, the sunshine dried out the trenches. The warmth gave the men a sense of security and contentment. And, too, they could sit back in their trenches and watch a new kind of war being fought in the air above them. Sometimes, when groups of Allied aircraft were locked in dogfights with their German adversaries, the engagement seemed like a football game, with the men in the opposing lines of trenches cheering or jeering the action overhead. The men on the ground did not realize that the outcome of each air battle could have a very direct effect on their welfare. The Spads and Fokkers gyrating above them were attempting to protect the observation planes and balloons which were patrolling No Man's Land from the sky. The slow-moving scout planes and the immobile hydrogen-filled balloons were sitting ducks for the victor of the battle between the pursuit planes.

By the time the United States entered the war, aerial observation had grown into a truly valuable military tool. From his wicker "car" beneath the balloon, an observer could direct artillery fire by telephone connected directly to the artillery battery and, with the same telephone, the observer could report any troop or supply movement within range of his binoculars. The use of radio permitted observation airplanes to penetrate the sky over enemy-held territory and report everything that went on beneath them. When the war reached a stalemate after the first battle of the Marne, the observation planes were equipped with cameras. By taking pictures of the same areas day after day and comparing them, the intelligence officers were able to discern changes in troop locations, new artillery positions, and the location of supply points. Once they were located, they became fair game for the artillery and for the crude bomber aircraft which could deliver destruction beyond the range of artillery.

Of course, the aerial observers with their field glasses and cameras had two serious disadvantages: They were blind at night; and they could not get close enough to the enemy to identify the units and judge their ability to fight. Consequently, the scouts of No Man's Land still had some nasty chores to perform.

On the night of May 18, 1918, the 166th Infantry sent a

patrol under the command of Lieutenant John Leslie across No Man's Land and into the town of Hau de Ancerviller. Leslie and three men were to hide themselves in the town and spend the day there, gathering whatever intelligence they could about the condition of German defenses in the area. They crawled "over the top" at eleven o'clock that night and reached a patch of willows at the edge of the town at about three in the morning. Leslie felt that it was too light to permit them to go all the way into the town, so they concealed themselves in the willows and surveyed their surroundings. In the course of the day they located three machine gun positions, an artillery battery, and the path taken by a German sentry with a dog. They marked the locations of wire entanglements and noted that many of them contained only one strand of barbed wire, an indication that the Germans must be short of wire. By sounds they heard, they were able to determine that three supply trains passed through Hau de Ancerviller that day. A wagon train was seen bringing supplies late in the afternoon, and in the early evening, a brass band serenaded the Germans in the trenches. Leslie and his men stayed in their hideout until ten o'clock that night, then made their way back to the American lines without having been seen or fired upon.

The report of this patrol made higher headquarters interested in determining just what the Germans were up to in the Hau de Ancerviller area. On the night of May 20 a larger patrol was sent out to enter the enemy trenches and bring back prisoners. The patrol was commanded by Lieutenant Milton Monnett. He took two sergeants, twenty men, and a pair of automatic rifles to provide fire support if they became heavily engaged.

Almost immediately they encountered a three-man German patrol which ran away in the direction of the road between Domèvre and Hau de Ancerviller. The Americans gave chase, hoping to make a quick capture, but were unable to catch up with the Germans. They encountered five Germans laying what appeared to be telephone wire. Since the wire crew seemed to be working their way toward them, the Americans lay in wait, again hoping to make an easy capture. Gradually Lieutenant Monnett moved his men to surround the Germans, but just as they were about to spring their trap, they saw a German patrol of about thirty men, pulling a heavy machine gun on wheels, heading in their direction. At the same time, Monnett heard imitated bird calls coming from several directions along his flanks and to the rear. While he had been trying to surround the German working party, a larger group of Germans had been in the process of surrounding him and his men!

Monnett deployed his men in skirmish formation and began to fall back toward the American lines. Now they saw another German patrol of about sixteen men on their right flank. They continued to fall back, but ran into still another group of Germans between them and the gap in the American wire. Monnett knew he would have to fight his way to safety and ordered his patrol to open fire on the Germans who were blocking their escape. The Germans took cover in some old foxholes and returned the fire. The patrol crawled close to the foxholes and dropped concussion grenades in on top of the Germans, leaving them either dead or semi-conscious. As Lieutenant Monnett's men continued to retreat, they grabbed the inert forms of two Germans from the foxholes and dragged them through the wire. Although he had not done the job in the way he had planned, Monnett had gotten his prisoners without losing a man.

The American patrol estimated that they had encountered about seventy Germans in all, and the prisoners told them that their own mission had been to cut the American wire. The location of the various German elements, coupled with the other intelligence, indicated that Monnett and his men had stumbled on a sizable German raiding party which had probably set out with the same purpose—to get into enemy trenches and bring back a prisoner.

A week later the Germans began what was to be their last major offensive. They attacked the French, British, and Americans along a front from Soissons west to Cantigny and northward to Arras. A separate attack was made against the British, Belgians, and Americans near Ypres in a final effort to break through to the Channel ports. The Allies were forced back all along the line. It seemed almost certain that the Germans would capture Paris.

On May 31 the Germans reached the banks of the Marne River for a second time, but further advance was blocked at Belleau Wood by the heroic defense of a brigade of United States Marines. Several fresh United States Army infantry divisions were sent to relieve exhausted French troops at Château Thierry. They held the German attack in that sector and then counterattacked to break the German momentum. Paris was saved, and by late July American manpower had swelled the Allied armies enough to permit an offensive all along the front.

The Germans clung tenaciously to an area around the little town of St. Mihiel. They had captured the area early in 1914 and had converted it into a complex fortress. As the Allied armies advanced on both sides of St. Mihiel, the area became a salient, protruding into the Allied lines like a knife. After much negotiating with Marshall Foch, the Supreme Allied Commander, who wanted the American divisions scattered all along the front, General Pershing got permission to assemble an all-American army for an attack on the salient. Fourteen American divisions, supported by a huge assemblage of American, British, and French artillery, attacked the St. Mihiel salient on September 12, 1918, and drove the Germans from the redoubt they had held for four years. From the English Channel to the Swiss border the Germans were irretrievably in retreat.

For the first time since they arrived in France, American scouts could operate according to military preference and national tradition. Patrols roamed the hills and woods searching for the fleeing Germans and giving warning whenever the enemy seemed to be preparing to make a stand. Communications were difficult to maintain. There were no lightweight radios that could be carried on patrols. The parties usually started out carrying reels of telephone wire which they rolled out as they went along, but as the situation became more fluid, they usually ran out of wire in a matter of hours. A few carrier pigeons could be taken along on a patrol, but with the whole Allied army on the move, they could not be relied upon to find their home bases. Daring scouts sometimes used captured German motorcycles or horses to get information back to their units. Therefore, though the patrols found the Germans and got plenty of information the American commanders needed, the transmission of the information was uncertain at best.

By early October the hopelessness of the military situation was apparent to the German High Command. A new chancellor was appointed with instructions to seek an armistice, but Kaiser Wilhelm was not willing to consider defeat inevitable. He left Berlin and went to the front to be with his armies, in some vain hope that his presence would inspire them. But the army had had more punishment than it could stand, and Marshal von Hindenburg joined the chancellor in asking the kaiser to abdicate. Marshall Foch gave the Germans the Allied armistice terms on November 8, and Kaiser Wilhelm fled into Holland on November 10. At the eleventh hour of the eleventh day of the eleventh month of 1918 the First World War came to an end. The Americans returned to their homes and divorced themselves from world affairs for another twenty-three years.

10

Patrolling the World

When the United States entered World War II in 1941 it faced two major enemies—Germany in Europe and Japan in the Pacific. To meet these two threats, American forces were spread around the world. The United States had never before put so many fighting men into the field. Never before had Americans faced such a wide variety of challenges from their enemies or from the environments in which they faced each other. The process of "searching out the land" had to be modified to each set of circumstances.

The American "island hopping" campaign, designed to force the Japanese back across the Pacific Ocean, began with the landing on Guadalcanal in the Solomon Islands in August 1942. During the next eighteen months, American forces in the Pacific grew in strength, and by February 1944, General Douglas MacArthur was ready to make a long jump toward the west. First, though, he needed to locate and secure a base which would support his burgeoning ground, naval, and air forces. On the map, the islands of Los Negros and Manus in the Admiralties looked like logical choices for that new base. There were two Japanese airfields on the islands, and the northwest reach of Los Negros formed Seeadler Harbor, one of the best deep-water anchorages in the Pacific. The general ordered a series of reconnaissance actions to determine the Japanese strength and dispositions on the Admiralties. Three of the aerial reconnaissance reports follow:

> 23 February, 1944: Momote and Lorengau strips appeared unserviceable. Nil activity. Nil new aircraft. Nil unusual signs of activity in entire Admiralty Islands.
> 24 February, 1944: Aircraft flew low but nil antiaircraft fire encountered. Nil signs of enemy activity. The island appears deserted.
> 26 February, 1944: . . . Villages on Los Negros Island appear deserted and roads have not been used lately. Damage in Lorengau town has not been repaired. No activity of any kind observed.

General MacArthur wanted Los Negros with its excellent Seeadler Harbor and airfield and he wanted them taken quickly. So far, reconnaissance had developed conflicting reports about Japanese strength on that island and on the adjoining larger island of Manus. Lieutenant General George C. Kenney, the commander of the air forces in the southwest Pacific area, argued that his reconnaissance aircraft had proved that there were no significant numbers of Japanese on either island. Major General Charles Willoughby, the G-2 (intelligence officer) of the command, estimated that about four thousand Japanese were on the islands and that, because Manus was separated from Los Negros by a very narrow channel, the Japanese on Manus could readily reinforce those on Los Negros.

One last attempt was made to solidify the intelligence situation. After midnight on February 27, a navy Catalina flying boat took aboard six members of the Alamo Scouts, a hand-picked group of men who were trained to operate independently for weeks at a time, often in "spitting" range of the Japanese. They could make themselves understood in the many native dialects and were skilled at organizing natives to work against the Japanese. Just after six o'clock on the morning of the twenty-seventh, the Catalina rendezvoused with a flight of B-25 bombers over Los Negros. While the bombers attacked all likely hiding places on the island, the Catalina landed and launched the scouts in a rubber raft. They paddled ashore near the island's southeast tip.

Almost immediately the scouts discovered that the area extending inland from Momote Point was infested with Japanese troops who were dug into well-concealed shelters under the cover of palm trees. The scouts radioed to the Catalina, "The Momote area is lousy with Japs."

Backing away from possible discovery by Japanese sentries, the Alamo Scouts made rapid notes of the defensive positions and the precise area of the Japanese encampment, called the Catalina by radio, and then paddled their rubber raft back out to sea to be picked up.

When General Kenney heard that the scouts' report contradicted his aerial reconnaissance reports, he belittled its accuracy, claiming that the scouts had been misled by what they saw and heard. A mere twenty-five Japanese, the general claimed, could have created the impression that there were actually hundreds present.

If the disagreement between his air commander and his intelligence officer upset General MacArthur, he did not show it. He still wanted Los Negros in a hurry. He decided to employ yet another form of scouting—a reconnaissance in force. He directed a force of about one thousand men to make a landing on Los Negros and to press their attack across the island. If the Japanese were not present in any sizable numbers, this force could handle them and secure the island. If, as General Willoughby estimated, there were major Japanese combat units available to defend the island, the reconnaissance force would dig in and try to defend whatever part of the island they were able to occupy. If things got really bad, they would withdraw to the beach and be evacuated. The unit that would make this reconnaissance was a squadron of the Fifth United States Cavalry, which seventy-six years earlier had been guided into combat with the Cheyenne and the Sioux by Buffalo Bill Cody.

These cavalrymen would fight on foot, of course, and they would be reinforced by light artillery, heavy antiaircraft machine guns, and a small group of naval officers and men who would direct the gunfire of ships standing offshore. They would be taken to Los Negros on board destroyers and would not take anything with them that could not be dismantled and carried ashore by hand.

The force was in position for a landing on February 29, just two days after the Alamo Scouts had rendered their disputed report. General MacArthur himself accompanied the invasion force and was standing on the bridge of the cruiser *Phoenix* when the ships opened fire at 7:40 A.M. The guns of thirteen destroyers and two cruisers pounded the targets that had been plotted by the Alamo Scouts. The time for the small landing craft to head for the beach inside Hyane Harbor was set for 8:15 A.M. This was to be known as H-Hour.

As H-Hour approached, the boats moved toward the "line of departure," an imaginary line in the water across which they were to charge in coordinated formation. Precisely at 8:15 the coxswain on the leading landing craft opened his throttle wide and roared through the harbor entrance. The covey of landing craft was immediately taken under fire by Japanese 20mm guns, but the lead boat charged through it and dropped its ramp on the sand of Los Negros at 8:17, just two minutes after it had crossed the line of departure.

Second Lieutenant Marvin Henshaw was the first man ashore. He was greeted by the sight of a panic-stricken Japanese machine gun crew, scarcely twenty yards away.

Henshaw dropped to one knee and aimed his carbine at one of the Japanese, by now running wildly for cover. Henshaw's first shot downed the Japanese, and a shot by one of Henshaw's men dropped a second. There were no casualties among the cavalry troopers in the first wave of boats.

By 9:00 o'clock three waves of troopers had landed and had pushed more than three hundred yards inland against very light opposition. Brigadier General William Chase, who commanded the reconnaissance force, radioed to the command ship, "enemy situation undetermined." By 9:50 o'clock the cavalrymen had overrun the entire airstrip. They found it covered with weeds, littered with the decaying wrecks of aircraft, and pitted with water-filled bomb craters. By noon the entire force was ashore and only five Japanese had been killed. It began to look as if General Kenney and his aerial scouts had been mostly correct.

But patrolling cavalrymen soon found signs that the enemy had been there in strength only a little earlier. They found a field kitchen with its fires still warm, and stacks of food supplies showed that the kitchen had fed a large number of men. A document they captured indicated that the area was defended by two hundred Japanese antiaircraft artillerymen. At 4:00 P.M. General MacArthur came ashore in the midst of a tropical rainstorm and awarded Lieutenant Henshaw the Distinguished Service Cross. After a brief look around he admonished General Chase "to remain here and hold the airstrip at any cost."

General Chase immediately decided that he could not defend a perimeter around the entire airstrip against expected counterattacks. He ordered his men to pull back toward the east and set up a shorter perimeter that could be more easily defended. While the Americans were scratching out their foxholes in preparation for a long night, the Japanese commander, Colonel Yoshio Ezaki, was issuing orders to Captain Baba of the First Battalion, 229th Infantry, to "annihilate the enemy who have landed. This is not a delaying action. Be resolute to sacrifice your life for the Emperor and commit suicide in case capture is imminent." As soon as darkness settled over the island, Captain Baba's men began to infiltrate the American position.

While Baba's main attack was being made against the southern part of the cavalry perimeter, other Japanese put on life preservers and swam across the harbor to attack the small group of artillerymen near the beach. Others managed to cut all the telephone wire strung between the American command posts. The troopers stayed in their cramped foxholes and fired at everything that moved. By sunrise the infiltration had stopped. Sixty-six dead Japanese were found in the American position. Seven cavalrymen were killed during the night.

On the second day, March 1, the cavalrymen patrolled outward from their perimeter, but were seldom able to move more than four hundred yards before encountering stiff enemy resistance. The previous night's fighting had shown that Los Negros was, in fact, "lousy with Japs." General MacArthur issued orders to move the rest of the Fifth Cavalry Regiment and additional support troops to the island as soon as possible. They arrived on the morning of March 2 and began to reinforce the perimeter. Colonel Ezaki had been doing a little patrolling of his own, and when he saw the American reinforcements coming ashore, he began to call for help from Japanese units in the interior of Manus Island. But they were slow in arriving and the Americans suffered little more than harassment during the night of March 2–3.

The delay in assembling his reinforcements proved militarily fatal for Colonel Ezaki. By the time he launched new attacks on the night of March 3–4, the cavalrymen had prepared their defenses carefully and had brought a complete battalion of artillery ashore. Japanese patrols began probing the American lines just at dusk. The Japanese pressure against the perimeter gradually increased until they began a frontal assault, not creeping along the ground as they had done on previous nights, but walking upright and talking and singing as they advanced to almost certain death. This continued throughout the night. The Japanese showed great determination and courage, but their attacks were not well coordinated. Pressure was never applied against more than one point in the American perimeter at any one time. An hour before dawn a last attack was made, and the troopers were so tired they were convinced that they heard the Japanese singing "Deep in the Heart of Texas" as they marched out to join their ancestors. At daylight a surviving Japanese officer and twelve enlisted men walked out into the open in front of Lieutenant Henshaw's platoon. The officer pulled the pin from a grenade and held it against his stomach. One by one the enlisted men followed suit. Thirteen muffled explosions were followed by a frightening silence.

Within a few days the entire First Cavalry Division was ashore and spreading out to seize the remaining islands of the Admiralty group. The Japanese put up a determined resistance against inevitable defeat, but by May 15 the islands were cleared and the development of a new base was well on its way. Captured Japanese records proved General Willoughby's intelligence estimate had been amazingly accurate: There had been 4,300 Japanese troops on Los Negros and Manus when the reconnaissance in force began on February 29. The Americans never knew how many Japanese casualties were carried away to be buried, but in the course of the fighting, they found 3,280 dead enemy soldiers and captured only 75.

While the men of the Fifth Cavalry were clearing the Admiralties, a very unusual group of American soldiers was combing the jungles and mountains of Burma, some four thousand miles to the northwest. These were the men of the 5307th Composite Unit (Provisional)—usually known by their much more glamorous name of Merrill's Marauders.

By May 1942 the Japanese had completed their conquest of Southeast Asia. In the process they had cut the Burma Road, the last overland supply route to China, and were menacing India. The Allies began an airlift of supplies into China "over the hump" of the Himalaya Mountains, but this was a very expensive and inefficient operation. The Burma Road had to be reopened if the Chinese armies were to provide any sort of effective resistance against the Japanese invaders.

When the Allied leaders met at Quebec, Canada, in August of 1943, they made the decision to provide a special American combat unit to assist the Chinese and British in retaking Burma. This unit would have only three thousand men but they would be hand-picked for their experience in jungle fighting. Their mission was to make long-range penetrations behind Japanese lines, attack vital Japanese installations, and disrupt their communications. While the Americans were confusing the Japanese, the Chinese forces would be attacking to clear the enemy from Burma.

The 5307th arrived in Bombay, India, on October 31, 1943. They immediately moved to a jungle training area near Deogarh where they were organized into three battalions of approximately one thousand men each. Each battalion was, in turn, divided into two combat teams, identified by the name of a color. Thus the First Battalion had the Red and White Combat Teams, the Second Battalion had the Blue and Green Combat Teams, and the Third Battalion had the Orange and Khaki Combat Teams. While at Deogarh they became accustomed, so far as was possible, to the rigors of the Asian jungles and hardened themselves for the long foot marches which lay ahead of them. The few heavy supplies and weapons that they would take with them would be carried by mules. Everything else would be carried on their backs, and they would be resupplied by parachute drop whenever necessary. If they had casualties, the only way to evacuate them would be to hack a small landing strip out of the jungle and call for a small L-4 spotter plane (a Piper Cub) to make the dangerous pickup.

Brigadier General Frank D. Merrill took command of the 5307th while it was in training, and early in January 1944 he led his men toward Ledo, Burma. The one-thousand-mile trip took a month by railroad and boat, with the last one hundred miles made on foot at the rate of ten miles per day. By February 19 they had reached their advance base at Ningbyen.

The area in which the marauders were to operate ranged from the muddy delta of the tributaries of the Irrawaddy River to the southern ranges of the Himalayas, more than ten thousand feet high. In between these extremes there were lesser mountains and every form of vegetation from swampy jungles to tangled rain forest with hardwood trees twenty-five feet in diameter and over a hundred feet tall. Although they would start their operations during the "dry" season, the weather would become increasingly hot and humid after March until the monsoon began sometime in June. Then would come from 150 to 250 inches of rain!

Although the mission assigned to General Merrill was essentially one of fighting the Japanese, the marauders had to find the enemy before they could fight him. For this reason each of the combat teams was organized with an intelligence and reconnaissance (I&R) platoon to scout for the enemy and to find routes through the jungle. From the very outset of marauder operations, the I&R platoons made the first contacts with the enemy and became involved in some of the wildest actions.

On March 4 the marauders were moving southwest through the Hukawng Valley toward the town of Walawbum. Their mission was to force the Japanese to abandon the town and the supplies they had stored there. Also, since the town was located at a critical junction on the only road through the area, they hoped to be able to cut off the Japanese troops that were farther north. The Orange and Khaki Combat Teams of the Third Battalion were working their way through the jungle east of the town, with the I&R platoon of the Orange team screening to the front and on the right flank. The Japanese had been reacting strangely to the advance of the marauders, and the Americans began to realize that the enemy was confused about the direction from which they were being attacked and also were uncertain about the size of the American force. In their confusion, the Japanese concentrated for a counterattack against the Orange I&R platoon, mistaking it for the main force.

Fortunately, Lieutenant Logan Weston, the I&R platoon leader, realized what was happening and was able to withdraw the platoon to the crest of a small hill and to establish an all-around defense. Weston realized, however, that his men could not hold out indefinitely. Carrying three seriously wounded scouts as gently as they could, the marauders withdrew toward the Orange Combat Team position with one squad forming a skirmish line to protect their retreat.

The Japanese made probing attacks against Orange Combat Team for two more days but then withdrew toward the south. The marauders were relieved by a Chinese regiment and began a brief rest period. There had been 2,750 Americans in the unit when the operation began. Only 8 had been killed; 37 were wounded. Still, because of the inroads of malaria and other sicknesses, there were just 2,500 marauders left in fighting condition.

The rest period lasted just four days. Then the marauders were ordered to penetrate fifteen to twenty miles behind Japanese lines to cut off supply routes and to harass their rear areas. The penetration required a circuitous march of more than fifty miles from their base at Walawbum, along narrow trails and over several high mountain ridges. The troops could make only two or three miles a day, hacking their way along trails which had become overgrown with vines and brush. The fifty-mile ordeal took almost two weeks.

On March 14 the I&R platoon of White Combat Team was cautiously working its way along the trail several miles ahead of the main body of troops when they came upon some footprints. The feet that had made the prints had worn form-fitting rubber shoes with a split big toe, a style used

Merrill's Marauders, early in the Burma campaign, rest beside a trail that had been cut through the dense jungle

only by Japanese. Lieutenant Samuel Wilson cautioned his platoon to be especially alert and sent his lead scout, Private John Sukup, ahead to act as the point of the platoon. For two hours the platoon followed the footprints down the trail, watching them grow continually fresher. Every turn in the trail brought a moment of suspense. Would they run head-long into an ambush or find their point man in the middle of the trail with his throat cut? The suspense was ended by a burst of fire somewhere ahead of them. Only a Thompson submachine gun (a "tommy gun") made a sound like that and Scout Sukup had one.

Sam Wilson ordered the platoon to hold fast while he ran forward to find Sukup. The scout was crouched at the side of the trail scanning the jungle. He told Wilson that he had almost fallen over an enemy soldier as he had rounded a bend. Sukup had fired at the running target but had missed.

Wilson brought the rest of the platoon forward and deployed them in a semicircle on both sides of the trail. He could already hear movement in the vegetation ahead of them. When the men were in position, Wilson had a Chinese interpreter call out and ask the people in the jungle to identify themselves. An answer was given, but only in the form of one word of Chinese, spoken uncertainly: "Wah . . . ? Wah . . . Wah . . . ?" The speaker obviously was not Chinese. "Fire!" The automatic rifles and tommy guns of the I&R platoon sent a hail of bullets whistling through the tangled jungle, and an answering volley was returned. The scouts had found the enemy.

Sam Wilson figured his job was done for the moment. He and his scouts crawled back to the main body of the combat team to make their report, pausing only long enough to send an occasional burst in the direction of the enemy.

The mission of the White Combat Team was to reach the town of Shaduzup and establish a roadblock on the Kamaing Road at that point. The Japanese party they encountered on the trail, however, proved so tenacious and obstructive that the combat team was forced to make their way around them through the jungle. This slowed progress to a snail's pace. The men doing the exhausting work of hacking a trail through the vines and brush had to be relieved every few minutes. The combat team had very little food, and the scarcity of streams in this upland area forced them to go without water for days at a time. The mules suffered as much as the men and gradually grew weaker. At times it seemed that it would be easier for the men to abandon the mules and carry the heavy equipment themselves rather than to push and pull the poor animals over every hill.

The going got a little easier as the White Combat Team began to descend into the valley of the Chengun River. Once into the valley, the men followed the river itself. Sam Wilson and his scouts explored every bend in the river, just as they had done on the trail. John Sukup would wade ahead of the platoon to a bend, scan the next stretch, and give the all-clear signal to Wilson. Sam would then move up to Sukup, verify the scout's observation, and then bring the rest of the platoon forward as Sukup moved on to the next bend. Gradually the river got wider, and the jungle canopy overhead slowly parted to admit the sunlight. Sukup turned a bend and looked out on a broad expanse of open river. Almost at the same instant he heard the braying of a mule—not behind him, where it should have been, but beyond the open water. He signaled Wilson forward, and together they listened to the sound of voices speaking a strange language, laughing and banging pots. Sam Wilson sent a runner back to the combat team and set up the rest of the platoon in outposts hidden along the river bank.

When the main body of White Combat Team closed up to the scouts, Wilson and Lieutenant Colonel William Osborn, who commanded the First Battalion of the marauders, crept forward and watched Japanese soldiers throw grenades into the river to kill fish for their dinner. Wilson and Osborn could hear more sounds from the other side of the river, but they could not tell what was going on. Wilson volunteered to cross the river to scout the situation. Osborn knew that the I&R platoon leader had been suffering from dysentery for weeks and that what little food he ate was almost immediately vomited, but the disposition of the enemy on the other side of the river had to be determined. He reluctantly let the lieutenant go with one other scout.

Wilson and Sergeant Perlee Tintary waded the river, holding their weapons over their heads, and rolled into the protective foliage on the far side just as a two-man Japanese patrol passed on a path above them. Their hearts pounding, they waited until the Japanese had passed farther down the trail, and then began to make their way in the direction of the sounds they had heard. After several hundred yards, they almost stumbled into a large bivouac area which lay astride the Kamaing Road. A large number of storage sheds, all apparently full of supplies, indicated the size and importance of the camp. After making careful notes of the camp layout, Wilson and Tintary worked their way back to the river and waded across, again just ahead of a passing Japanese patrol.

Shaking from a combination of fear, cold, and sickness, Sam Wilson made his report to Colonel Osborn. The colonel at once set up plans for a night attack on the Japanese camp. The attack was most successful. The Japanese lost more than three hundred men killed, while the marauders lost only eight. Best of all, the hungry men gorged themselves on everything they found in the Japanese storehouses, even eating eggs raw rather than waiting to cook them.

The battle at Shaduzup had taken place on March 28. By mid-May the marauders had participated in many other operations deep in enemy-held territory, climaxing their operations with the seizure of the vital airfield at Myitkyina, the largest town in the interior of Burma. This last effort drained the marauders to an extent that left them unable to carry on effectively. Of the almost 3,000 men who had started the campaign, only 1,310 were able to participate in the assault on Myitkyina. When that battle was over, only 631 men were still on their feet and many of them were too weak to fight. By this time, however, the tide of battle in Burma had turned in favor of the Allies, and the reason for the existence of the marauders had disappeared. The 5307th Composite Unit was disbanded in August 1944.

The year 1944 was probably the busiest one during the course of World War II. It had taken the United States almost two years to mobilize and to get enough forces into the field to tip the scales in favor of the nations allied against the Germans and the Japanese. Mid-1944 saw those scales inclining more noticeably. The Japanese were being slowly forced out of Southeast Asia and the relentless pressure of American land and sea power had spread Allied control over the vast expanse of the Pacific. Rome fell to combined British and American forces on June 4. Just two days later, an armada of four thousand ships and landing craft set out from England, crossed the choppy waters of the English Channel, and landed an invading army on the shores of Normandy. Adolf Hitler's *Festung Europa* (Fortress Europe) received its greatest blow on June 6, 1944—D-Day.

There had been very little actual scouting of the Normandy beaches before the invasion. One of the most important parts of the invasion plan was the deception of the German intelligence agencies. There would have been too great a risk of destroying the element of surprise if detailed reconnaissance had been conducted on the beaches. Instead, there had been some random raids by British Commandos with a combined mission of destroying German installations and gathering a limited amount of intelligence, and the Allied air forces had photographed likely invasion sites along the channel coast of France almost daily for months. At the same time, false radio signals had been transmitted to confuse the Germans about the disposition of allied units and, most important, about the true location of the invasion area. Even the bombardment of the beaches was held off until the very last minute so the Germans could not move reinforcements to Normandy in time to meet the invading Allies.

Although it seems unfair to single out one unit as a vehicle for discussing the invasion of Normandy, the Sixteenth Infantry Regiment, one of the three regiments assigned to the First Infantry Division, probably suffered more from the lack of detailed scouting and precise location of enemy defenses than any comparable unit in the invasion force.

H-Hour for the invasion of Normandy was 6:30 A.M., June 6. The Sixteenth Infantry was to land with its Second and Third battalions abreast on two parts of Omaha Beach known as "Fox Green" and "Easy Red." The First Battalion was to be in reserve initially, but was to pass through the other two battalions as soon as they had established themselves and secured their parts of the beachhead.

Things went badly almost from the beginning. Thirty-two specially equipped tanks were to have preceded the infantry to the beach to act as mobile pillboxes and to assault enemy gun positions. Twenty-six of the tanks went straight to the bottom when they were launched from their landing craft in water that was too deep. As soon as the landing craft carrying the troops came into range, they were attacked by German antitank guns and machine guns which had not been touched by the naval and air bombardment. Boats were sunk, and other boats rammed into the submerged hulks or got hung up on obstacles concealed under the water. Soon the water was filled with men struggling to stay afloat in their life jackets under the weight of their equipment. Soon, too, the inert forms of the dead were gathered on the beaches, and the living hid behind them, their only cover from the murderous fire from the overlooking cliffs. Boats landed at the wrong beaches, and officers found they were either commanding men from other units or no men at all.

Gradually, the men worked their way across the sand and under the protection of the cliffs. They were screened from enemy fire, but they could not move either forward or backward. Wounded men lay out on the sand, and many more men were wounded trying to drag them to cover. Weapons were clogged with sand and had to be taken apart and cleaned—not an easy job under those circumstances. Finally, however, a semblance of organization began to appear. It took five organized frontal assaults on enemy strong points, but the Sixteenth Infantry finally opened the only exit from the beach for an entire corps. They held it for forty-eight hours in the face of five counterattacks. In those forty-eight hours the regiment lost 971 men. The questions will always remain: What would it have been like if the landing had been more deliberate; if we really had known how deep the water was and exactly where the obstacles were; and if the navy and air corps had been able to take the time to really soften up the beach?

For some of the Allied invasion forces, the process of moving inland from the beachhead started almost immediately, but the remaining men of the Sixteenth Infantry were largely out of action for more than a month as they gradually built up to strength again. When the key town of St. Lô was taken on July 18, the Allies and the reconstructed Sixteenth Infantry were ready to break out of the beachhead and make a dash across France. Unfortunately, a succession of rainy days curtailed the preparatory bombing attacks, and the general offensive toward the east was delayed for a week. By then the Germans had been able to bring up supplies and had prepared defensive positions.

American infantry and armor leaped forward on July 25. The Eighth Corps of General George S. Patton's Third Army broke the enemy line at Avranches and hurtled south into Brittany. The roaring tanks of the Fourth Armored Division overcame German resistance by sheer force of firepower and armored momentum. By August 1 the division had fought its way fifty miles to the south and into the city of Rennes, but in doing so had developed a very badly exposed left flank. The Second Cavalry Group (Mechanized) was committed to the role of screening the exposed flank to make sure that the advancing armored division would have warning of any German threats to that flank.

The mission of screening for an advancing force is a traditional one for the cavalry. In previous major European wars and in the American Civil War, the cavalry always rode on the flanks of the armies to provide security and intelligence. In this war, the cavalry was mounted in light tanks and armored cars, but although the sound of galloping horses had been replaced by the roaring of engines, the dashing spirit of the cavalry was still very much in evidence. The Second Cavalry Group commander dispatched one of his units, the Second Cavalry Reconnaissance Squadron, with the mission, "Reconnoiter to the southeast in the zone of St. Aubin du Comier—Fougères."

The reconnaissance was uneventful until C Troop clattered into Fougères at daylight on August 3. The Germans had not abandoned the town, and they took a dim view of having their sleep disturbed. A German "88" antitank gun scored a direct hit on the lead scout car, wounding the troop commander, and the rest of the cars immediately went into reverse, backing out of town as quickly as possible. The remaining officers decided that they would report the presence of determined defenders in Fougères, and then move on. The town was cleaned out the next day by the Seventy-ninth Infantry Division, which followed C Troop into Fougères.

This incident illustrates how the cavalry scouts operated. They would approach each road junction, every bridge, and every town cautiously, feel their way through it, across it, or over it, and then report their reconnaissance by radio as they moved on to the next likely point of German resistance. If they ran into the enemy, they would fight only hard enough to make the enemy commit themselves, then would back away and report the situation. Sometimes they had to fight to get away. One such incident occurred on August 5 in the town of Segré.

A platoon of Troop C, Forty-second Cavalry Reconnaissance Squadron (companion squadron of the Second Cavalry), under the command of Lieutenant George Lindoerfer, entered Segré under the cover of darkness and prowled through the town on foot looking for evidence of Germans. The platoon had moved about halfway through the town when German machine guns opened up on them from at least three hidden positions. The scouts threw themselves behind any available protection and began to worm their way back out of town.

Lieutenant Lindoerfer and his lead scout, Corporal William Pirone, were moving in front of a house as the firing started. The only available cover was behind two low steps up to the front door of the house, and Pirone got there first. Lindoerfer had to make the best of the scant protection offered by the gutter. As bullets whistled up and down the street, Pirone muttered to Lieutenant Lindoerfer, "Get up and run like hell for that alley back there! I'll cover you from here, then you cover me from the alley." The lieutenant grunted agreement with the plan. He was just preparing himself for a running leap to the alley when both he and Pirone became aware that the door to the house was opening!

Pirone pointed his tommy gun at the widening shadow of the doorway, expecting a burst of shots at any instant. The door opened a little wider, and a hand appeared holding a wine bottle with a glass inverted over the cork. The hand set the bottle down on the top step, inches from Pirone's face, then slowly withdrew into the shadows. It took the Americans a few moments to get over their surprise. Then Lindoerfer said, "O.K. Here I go!" and made his dash to the alley. Pirone followed with the wine, but dropped the glass as he ran. It tasted pretty good right out of the bottle.

During the balance of the summer and fall the Allies continued their race across France. Early in September the American First Army pushed through Luxembourg and pressed into the defense of the Siegfried Line along the German border. The momentum of the attack spent itself in several attempts to get through the Siegfried Line. One attempt to outflank it with an airborne invasion of the northern Netherlands proved to be a disaster. Forward progress stopped as winter set in.

While the Allies built up supplies and manpower for a final assault of the Siegfried Line, the German leader, Adolf Hitler, organized what he realized might well be a last desperate counteroffensive. Acting on Hitler's instructions, the field commander, Marshal von Rundstedt, massed three entire armies, more than 300,000 men, on a ninety-mile front opposite the Ardennes Forest.

The Ardennes is so thickly forested that the Allies had discounted the likelihood of a German attack there. It was defended by only token forces. On December 16 von Rundstedt's three-pronged attack swept through the forest and overran the defenders. The prong which von Rundstedt had intended as his main attack turned to the north and was beaten back after some initial success. The southern attack was stopped dead in its tracks, but the thrust through the center and into the lightly-manned American defenses carried fourteen miles on the first day. The Germans quickly surrounded the town of Bastogne and trapped thousands of American troops. Only the tenacity of the "Bloody Bastards of Bastogne"—the soldiers of the U.S. Army's 101st Airborne Division—prevented a German sweep to the Meuse River.

American infantry and armored divisions concentrated on the "bulge" in their lines as fast as they could get moving. Because of the plans for an Allied offensive, there was an unusually large number of units in reserve, all of which were ready for the attack. Heavy snows made movement difficult, and day after day of poor flying weather made air attacks against the Germans impossible, but the counterattacking Americans slowly closed in on von Rundstedt's armies.

Christmas got little notice that year. The snow was falling steadily and the men on both sides were fighting discomfort as well as each other. Both German and American patrols began wearing white snow capes over their uniforms so they would not be silhouetted against the snow. Trench foot and frostbite became common. A man could catch an ordinary cold one day and have pneumonia the next.

The skies over Western Europe finally cleared in the second week of January 1945. The long-delayed Allied offensive started on January 15. Hundreds of thousands of men—British, French, and American—moved on Germany from the north, south, and west. Scouts for these armies found crossing sites over the Roer River, paths through the demolished dikes of Holland, and gaps in the dragon's teeth of the Siegfried Line. Once it started to roll, the final great offensive in Europe did not stop until it reached Adolf Hitler's sanctuary high in the Bavarian Alps.

The Germans gave up on May 8, 1945. The Japanese, driven from island to island across the Pacific, were prepared for a final desperate defense of their home islands, but they were not prepared (and neither was the rest of the world) for the atomic holocausts at Hiroshima and Nagasaki. They surrendered on September 2, 1945.

American scouts had "searched out the land" of many continents and hundreds of islands. Never before had they been so severely challenged. Never before had they performed more admirably.

11

In the Best Tradition
of Rogers' Rangers

The years after World War II brought the United States more international responsibilities than the nation had ever faced before. Americans became leaders in the struggle to reestablish a world at peace. American money and American know-how helped to start Europe toward economic recovery and to build a sound, democratic government in Japan. The United States gave generous assistance to young nations sponsored by the United Nations.

Peace never really arrived, however. The Russians made puppet states of the Central European countries that fell under their domination at the end of the war. The Chinese communists and Chiang Kai-shek's nationalists, who had declared a moratorium on their fight for control of China in 1939 so they could fight the Japanese, renewed the struggle that had begun in 1927. Two years after World War II had ended there were two Chinas, one communist and the other ostensibly democratic.

The Communists' policy of expanding their influence wherever and whenever they could brought them increasingly into conflict with the United States, the only major democratic nation that had emerged from World War II

174

with enough power to influence the international chess game. Tensions slowly mounted, and the first serious armed clash occurred in Korea in the summer of 1950. Three years and 142,000 casualties later, the United Nations was able to negotiate a tenuous truce.

The fighting in Korea had not made use of any spectacular new tactics or weapons. The very nature of the land in Korea made large-scale movement difficult, and although there were periods of rapid movement up and down the peninsula, there was little opportunity for the wide-open kind of warfare used in Europe during World War II. The war, in fact, became more and more like a new staging of World War I, with the troops dug in and staring at each other across a stretch of No Man's Land.

Scouting that land turned out to be the same kind of dirty, very personal job that it had been in World War I. Patrols went out looking for specific information, but they had to rely on the cover of darkness to get close to an objective. Once there, they might not be able to see anything of the clever enemy. Patrolling rapidly degenerated to a prisoner-capturing operation and the prime mark of success of a patrol was to bring back an enemy officer. Decreasing amounts of credit were given for capturing a sergeant, a corporal, or an ordinary soldier. Although both sides questioned their prisoners at great length, it is doubtful that the amount of intelligence gained justified the risk taken in sending out the patrols. Many of them never returned.

The Korean War ended in the fall of 1953, and it appeared that peace had come to Asia. Unfortunately, the seed of another conflict had been planted in French Indochina at the end of World War II when the Viet Minh Front led by Ho Chi Minh tried to replace the defeated Japanese and keep the French from returning. "Uncle Ho," as he was called, rallied the Vietnamese people to fight the French colonials who had occupied Indochina for almost 150 years and who sought to reestablish control after the Japanese left. This revolt flared into large-scale warfare just as peace came to Korea. When the French were finally defeated at Dien Bien Phu in May 1954, Ho Chi Minh attempted to establish himself and the Viet Minh as the rulers of all of Vietnam. By this time, however, "Uncle Ho's" inclination toward Communism had become well known, and those Vietnamese who objected to a Communist-oriented regime attempted to get rid of him. A conference in Geneva, Switzerland, tried to negotiate a compromise solution to the problem by dividing the country in half. The Communists would rule the northern half and the anti-Communists would rule the southern half under the leadership of Ngo Dinh Diem, a devout Catholic. This uneasy arrangement lasted until 1957, when the Viet Minh began to send saboteurs and guerrillas into South Vietnam to disrupt the government and the economy. At the request of the South Vietnamese government, the United States sent a handful of military advisors to help train Vietnamese troops. The flow of guerrillas slowly increased until, by early 1961, there were about fifteen thousand Viet Cong (the name the southern Vietnamese gave to the Viet Minh) troops in the Republic of Vietnam.

President Diem could no longer cope with this growing interference from the North. Men and supplies were flowing southward down a complex of trails and rivers known as the "Ho Chi Minh Trail" faster than the government troops could deal with them. In December 1961, President Diem wrote to President Kennedy and asked for increased American military and economic assistance. At first the United States sent equipment, military advisors and helicopter units to help the Vietnamese troops fight the Viet Cong, but despite this, the flow down the Ho Chi Minh Trail increased. By 1963 there were twenty-two thousand Viet Cong in South

Vietnam. Diem was assassinated and his regime deposed in the first of a series of military coups, and the fighting grew in magnitude and ferocity.

Early in 1965 the number of Viet Cong in South Vietnam had risen to more than forty thousand, and the South Vietnamese, despite a veritable avalanche of economic assistance and steady growth in the number of American military advisors, were on the verge of catastrophe. In March, President Johnson ordered United States Marines to protect the city of Danang and its important air base in northernmost South Vietnam. In May, the 173d Airborne Brigade of the United States Army arrived at Bien Hoa, just outside the capital of Saigon. Within a few weeks paratroopers of the 173d were ranging the jungles looking for the Viet Cong.

The Americans soon found that the day-to-day business of fighting the Viet Cong added up to a series of fruitless patrols interspersed with an occasional exchange of shots with snipers. Only rarely were there engagements between sizable forces. On any one day in Vietnam the Americans and the South Vietnamese might conduct a total of one thousand patrols, only ten of which might make contact with the Viet Cong.

The Americans also learned that the Viet Cong were clever enemies. They knew the land in which they were operating, and they took advantage of their ability to mingle with the population without being easily detected. Although the Japanese had been excellent jungle fighters in World War II, they had lacked this camouflage. They did not look like the natives of the Pacific Islands or Indochina and they did not speak their languages. The Japanese had been as alien to the environment as their American adversaries. The Viet Cong, however, could simply hide their weapons and take on the guise of local natives.

The Japanese had also been clever in their use of concealment and in the way they had placed booby traps along jungle trails, but the Viet Cong made them look like amateurs. When they were hard-pressed for ammunition, the Viet Cong managed to take unexploded artillery shells and aerial bombs and turn them into death traps for patrols approaching their hiding places. When no explosives were available, or when they wanted to use a silent weapon, they would plant punji stakes of sharpened bamboo in concealed holes along the trails. The amazingly strong bamboo would go through the soles of the boots, or jab into the legs, of anyone who stepped into these traps. Although the wounds were seldom fatal, the Viet Cong often poisoned the tips of the bamboo with human excrement, causing an infection that could keep a scout out of action for a long time.

The men of the U.S. Army Special Forces had been among the first Americans to arrive in Vietnam when the call for help had gone out. Their mission had been to train the Vietnamese to patrol their borders and to guard against infiltration. The Green Berets of the Special Forces operated in small teams scattered in villages along the western border of South Vietnam from the seventeenth parallel (which divides North and South Vietnam) to the Gulf of Siam. Few of the natives along that border are true Vietnamese. They are Laotians, Cambodians, and tribesmen of the Montagnard and Rade clans. The men of the Special Forces learned their languages and gained their confidence by living among them. Soon they were able to organize the men into what was formally called the Civilian Irregular Defense Group but was usually known as the "Strikers." Operating with these natives, the Special Forces gained a great deal of knowledge about how the enemy fought. This knowledge was passed on to the regular combat units that began arriving in 1965. There is little doubt that the lessons learned by the Green Berets saved many lives.

A typical patrol from one of the Special Forces camps consisted of a platoon of Strikers and four Americans. Among the Americans were experts in skills designed to handle any situation—an intelligence expert, a radio operator, a medical aidman, and a team leader. Actually, any of the Green Berets could handle all of the jobs, since it was common practice for every Special Forces trooper to learn the entire range of skills, including a knowledge of enemy weapons and the ability to use explosives.

These border patrols acted as a sort of "early warning" system for the combat units. They provided the bulk of intelligence about movements of enemy units into South Vietnam from North Vietnam, Laos, and Cambodia. Once an enemy unit was discovered on the move, the patrol reported its location by radio and then discreetly followed along behind it or on its flank, reporting the course it was following. Of course, these small border patrols did their best to avoid direct contact with the enemy, but every now and then they were discovered and had to fight their way clear. In most cases they tried to make their way to a previously arranged pickup point for extraction by helicopters, but if they were pressed too hard, they would use the old trick of Rogers' Rangers and simply scatter into the jungle.

The helicopter added a new dimension to patrolling. In earlier wars, patrols were forced to move overland, either on foot or horseback or in some kind of a vehicle, running the risk of being detected before they reached the area in which the patrol was to be conducted. By loading a patrol into helicopters which could take a roundabout course to the patrol area, following rivers and valleys to keep below the skyline, they could be landed in any small clearing in a few seconds. The helicopters then sped away, following a different course. Unless the enemy happened to be very close to the landing site, he could not tell whether the helicopters had landed to drop off a patrol or had simply flown behind the screen of a tree line. Once the patrol objective was accomplished, the men rendezvoused with the helicopters at a prearranged time and place, or called them in by radio.

The use of the helicopter even brought about a new kind of scouting, the Long Range Reconnaissance Patrol. Once the border patrols of the Special Forces had given warning of an advancing enemy unit, the LRRP's from the combat units were sent out to continue the tracking process and to provide intelligence about the size of the force. The members of the LRRP's were all volunteers, hardened into the best possible physical condition and individually skilled in all aspects of patrolling. Every member of the patrol was taught how to adjust artillery fire and call in strikes by the armed army helicopters and fighter-bombers of the air force. Each man was taught to slide down a rope from a helicopter hovering one hundred feet above the ground— with his pack and all of his combat gear hanging on his back. As a team, they learned how to leap quickly from a helicopter hovering just above the ground so the enemy would not be sure whether anyone had been landed.

Not all of the LRRP's work was done in the jungle. One patrol from the Ninth Infantry Division, for example, was landed in the Mekong Delta region of Vietnam to look for a Viet Cong camp that was thought to be in the area. The next day the patrol was searching in the grassy marshes when it spotted a group of Viet Cong unloading mortar ammunition from a sampan. Staff Sergeant Arlyn Wieland, the team leader, realized that he and his men must have found the camp, but he knew that the patrol would not have accomplished its job until it had determined the size of the camp and the number of Viet Cong using it. He and his men settled down to spend the rest of the day in the cover of some heavy bush.

A member of the Long Range Reconnaissance Patrol rappels down a
nylon rope from a helicopter. This technique is used in the jungle

As darkness fell, Sergeant Wieland formed his men into a single file and set out to crawl through the marsh toward the enemy camp. Suddenly the point man dropped flat on the ground. The rest of the patrol followed his example and pressed flat into the mud. A column of khaki-clad Viet Cong passed within a few feet of the point man, talking and joking with each other, unaware of the presence of the American patrol. After a few minutes, the point man started moving forward again, but he had hardly moved a dozen feet when he again flattened himself into the ground. Another group of Viet Cong were coming directly toward them!

Sergeant Wieland frantically signaled his men to spread out to the left and right but to keep crawling ahead. Assisted by the deepening darkness, the patrol again avoided detection and made its way through the center of the enemy camp. They reached a little piece of high ground, and Sergeant Wieland deployed his men in a defensive pattern while he called in artillery and air strikes on the enemy. With the Viet Cong very much occupied in trying to protect themselves from the rain of shells, the patrol jogged unmolested down the trail to their pickup point. Within a few minutes they were in helicopters and on their way to the base camp.

The Long Range Reconnaissance Patrols became such a threat to the security of the Communist troops that they began to take extraordinary pains to locate and eliminate them. An LRRP from the 173d Airborne Brigade, operating from a base camp near Dak To in the central highlands of Vietnam, was the first reconnaissance unit to encounter enemy soldiers using scout dogs in an effort to locate the Americans. Staff Sergeant Edgar McNeal and his four scouts were flushed like a small covey of quail by two North Vietnamese regular soldiers with canine assistants. The North Vietnamese ran when they saw the Americans, and McNeal and his men gave chase, hoping to capture the enemy patrol before they could give a warning. The enemy got away, however, and McNeal was left with a hard decision. If they stayed there, the enemy would undoubtedly come looking for them and there would be an opportunity for the Americans to set up a good ambush before continuing with their patrol mission. If, on the other hand, they continued toward their patrol objective, the North Vietnamese might track them down with the dogs. They would have to fight sooner or later. McNeal decided to fight where they were, in a prepared position. In the meantime, just to play safe, he called the base camp and reported the situation. The base promised to have helicopters standing by in case a quick rescue became necessary.

McNeal's prediction proved to be correct. A short time later they heard the barking of dogs as the North Vietnamese scouts returned with reinforcements. As the sounds grew louder, the jungle was enveloped in the quick darkness of sunset. The patrol silently held its position, ready to spring an ambush on anyone who came down the trail toward them. But no one came down the trail. Instead, they heard noises behind them and to the right and left. In trying to trap the enemy they had been trapped themselves!

Fortunately, the only direction from which they could not hear any noise was a clearing where a helicopter could pick them up. They quietly assembled their equipment and started toward the clearing. A few yards down the trail the point man, Specialist James York, threw up his arm in the signal to halt. They froze in position as a group of North Vietnamese filed by not more than ten yards away. After a short wait, they started toward the clearing again, and the radio operator called the base at Dak To to send in the helicopters. The patrol reached the clearing but stayed hidden in the jungle until they heard the first helicopter overhead. By this time the enemy was closing in and beginning to fire at the helicopters. It was now so dark that the pilots could not make a safe landing in the small clearing, so they dropped ropes to the men waiting below. Two of the scouts pulled themselves up the ropes and into the helicopter before the enemy fire drove it away. A second 'copter tried to get into position to lower its ropes, but McNeal waved it away rather than risk having it shot down. McNeal and the two men who were still with him fired sporadically into the jungles to slow down any enemy soldiers who might be trying to sneak up on them. Bullets from enemy guns were whipping through the tall buffalo grass over their heads and cracking through the bamboo thicket on the edge of the clearing.

Unknown to Sergeant McNeal, the helicopter pilots had called for some armed helicopters to pin the enemy down while the extraction was completed. Under cover of the gunfire from the sky, a rescue helicopter got a rope down to the patrol radio operator and he scrambled up like an oversized monkey, carrying radio, pack, rifle, and all. Unfortunately, the armed helicopters ran out of ammunition at this point and had to return to Dak To to rearm. McNeal and his remaining scout could not stay in the clearing any longer. Using a flashlight, the sergeant signaled the orbiting rescue helicopter that they would try to move to another clearing. They began running through the jungle toward a small clearing a few hundred yards away. Their progress was unavoidably noisy and the enemy stayed hot on their heels.

The second clearing was hardly more than a narrow vertical tunnel between the gigantic hardwood trees. McNeal pointed the flashlight upward, praying the helicopter pilot could see its beam. He did. The ropes came down and the two men started to scramble upward as the enemy opened up with every weapon they had, even a bazooka. The helicopter pilot applied maximum power and pulled his ship straight up, with Sergeant McNeal and the other man still climbing hand-over-hand up the ropes. The armed helicopters returned to deliver a final dose of suppressive fire, but by that time the job was done. Five very tired scouts were on their way back to Dak To with their hearts still pounding in their throats.

As the long-range reconnaissance teams roamed the jungle, they encountered all sorts of strange situations and had to cope with them by using only the means they had brought along. One team from the First Cavalry Division was cautiously feeling its way through the jungle one day when it came face to face with a whole family of tigers—Papa, Mama, and two adolescent cats—all with mean dispositions and a definite curiosity about the strange two-legged creatures who had surprised them.

The patrol had plenty of firepower for dealing with the tigers, but shooting would have given away their position. Five of the six scouts beat a tactical retreat into the branches of a tree. The machine gunner decided he would just sit at the base of the tree. If one of the pussycats got obnoxious, his M-60 machine gun would discourage it.

Meanwhile, up in the tree Sergeant Ray Belfield, the patrol leader, was in earnest radio conversation with the base camp. He told the radio operator at the base that he and his men were trained to kill Viet Cong, not fool with pussycats. The radio operator solicited advice from the would-be tiger experts at the camp and relayed their suggestions. "Try barking like a dog . . . shoot them with tranquilizers . . . feed them poisoned meat" were a few of them. The machine gunner sitting at the bottom of the tree took more practical action. He lured Papa Tiger close enough and then squirted him in the face with insect repellent from an aerosol can. The big cat rubbed its face with a paw, let out a howl of discomfort, and loped off into the jungle with the whole family after him. The patrol continued on its way.

American fighting men have nurtured the scouts' traditions and skills for more than two hundred years. The advance of technology has had only limited influence on the ways in which a military commander gets his information about the enemy and the terrain. The airplane has lengthened the range to which the commander can extend his surveillance. Cameras and electronic devices, mounted on airplanes, can provide information about the location of enemy gun positions and can detect truck convoys moving under the cover of darkness. But if the commander wants to know what unit the guns are supporting, or precisely where that unit is located, he must once again place his trust in his scouts. From Rogers' Rangers to the Long Range Reconnaissance Patrols, the scouts have shown their skill, their courage, and their obedience to the challenging command, "Search out the land!"

Appendix

Rogers' "Plan of Discipline"

Following are the most important of the twenty-eight rules Robert Rogers drew up for his rangers, which are still the basis for the training of scouts in the United States Army.

Rule I   All Rangers are to be subject to the rules and articles of war; to appear at roll-call every evening on their own parade, equipped each with a firelock, sixty rounds of powder and ball, and a hatchet, at which time an officer from each company is to inspect the same, to see that they are in order, so as to be ready on an emergency to march at a minute's warning; and before they are dismissed the necessary guards are to be drafted, and scouts for the next day appointed.

Rule II   Whenever you are ordered out to the enemy's forts or frontiers for discoveries, if your number be small, march in single file, keeping at such a distance from each other as to keep one shot from killing two men, sending one man, or more, forward, and the like on each side, at the distance of twenty yards from the main body, if the ground you march over will admit of it to give the signal to the officer of the enemy, and of their number, &c.

Rule III   If you march over marshes or soft ground, change your position, and march abreast of each other, to prevent

187

the enemy from tracking you (as they would if you marched in a single file) till you get over such ground and then resume your former order, and march until it is quite dark before you encamp, which do, if possible, on a piece of ground that may afford your sentries the advantage of seeing or hearing the enemy at some considerable distance, keeping one half of your whole party awake alternately throughout the night.

Rule V   If you have the good fortune to take any prisoners, keep them separated till they are examined, and in your return take a different route from that in which you went out, that you may better discover any party in your rear, and have an opportunity, if their strength be superior to yours, to alter your course, or disperse, as circumstances may require.

Rule VII   If you are obliged to receive the enemy's fire, fall, or squat down, till it is over, then rise and discharge at them. If their main body is equal to yours, extend yourselves occasionally; but if superior, be careful to support and strengthen your flanking parties, to make them equal with theirs, that if possible you may repulse them to their main body . . .

Rule IX   If you are obliged to retreat, let the front of your whole party fire and fall back, till the rear has done the same, making for the best ground you can; by this means you will oblige the enemy to pursue you, if they do at all, in the face of a constant fire.

Rule X   If the enemy is so superior that you are in danger of being surrounded by them, let the whole body disperse, and take a different road to the place of rendesvous appointed for that evening, which must every morning be altered and fixed for the evening ensuing . . .

Rule XIII   In general, when pushed upon by the enemy, reserve your fire till they approach very near, which will then put them into greater surprise and the consternation, and give you an opportunity of rushing upon them with your hatchets and cutlasses to the better advantage.

Rule XIV When you encamp at night, fix your sentries in such a manner as not to be relieved from the main body till morning, profound secrecy and silence being often of the last importance in these cases. Each sentry therefore, should consist of six men, two of whom must be constantly alert, and when relieved by their fellows, it should be done without noise; and in case those on duty see or hear any thing, which alarms them, they are not to speak, but one of them is silently to retreat, and acquaint the commanding officer thereof, that proper dispositions may be made . . .

Rule XV At the first dawn of day, awake your whole detachment; that being the time when the savages choose to fall upon their enemies, you should by all means be in readiness to receive them.

Rule XVII Before you leave your encampment, send out small parties to scout around it, to see if there by any appearance or track of an enemy that might have been near you during the night.

Rule XVIII When you stop for refreshment, choose some spring or rivulet if you can, and dispose your party so as not to be surprised, posting proper guards and sentries at due distance, and let a small party waylay the path you came in, lest the enemy be pursuing.

Rule XIX If, on your return, you have to cross rivers, avoid the usual fords as much as possible, lest the enemy should have discovered, and be there expecting you.

Rule XXII When you return from a scout, and come near our forts, avoid the usual roads, and avenues thereto, lest the enemy should have headed you, and lay in ambush to receive you, when almost exhausted with fatigue.

Index

190

Printed in U.S.A.